# Pomeranians

**Marguerite Stocker**

*Pomeranians*

*Project Team*
Editor: Heather Russell-Revesz
Copy Editor: Ann Fusz
Design: Leah Lococo Ltd., Stephanie Krautheim
Series Design: Stephanie Krautheim

*T.F.H. Publications*
President/CEO: Glen S. Axelrod
Executive Vice President: Mark E. Johnson
Publisher: Christopher T. Reggio
Production Manager: Kathy Bontz

T.F.H. Publications, Inc.
One TFH Plaza
Third and Union Avenues
Neptune City, NJ 07753

*Discovery Communications, Inc. Book Development Team*
Maureen Smith, Executive Vice President & General
  Manager, Animal Planet
Carol LeBlanc, Vice President, Marketing and Retail
  Development
Elizabeth Bakacs, Vice President, Creative Services
Peggy Ang, Director, Animal Planet Marketing
Caitlin Erb, Marketing Associate

Printed and bound in China
06 07 08 09 10  1 3 5 7 9 8 6 4 2


Library of Congress Cataloging-in-Publication Data
Stocker, Marguerite.
Pomeranians / Marguerite Stocker.
p. cm. – (Animal Planet pet care library)
ISBN 0-7938-3752-9 (alk. paper)
1. Pomeranian dog. I. Animal Planet (Television network) II. Title. III. Series.
SF429.P8S76 2006
636.76–dc22
2006006369

This book has been published with the intent to provide accurate and authoritative information in regard to the subject matter within. While every precaution has been taken in preparation of this book, the author and publisher expressly disclaim responsibility for any errors, omissions, or adverse effects arising from the use or application of the information contained herein. The techniques and suggestions are used at the reader's discretion and are not to be considered a substitute for veterinary care. If you suspect a medical problem consult your veterinarian.

*The Leader In Responsible Animal Care For Over 50 Years!*™
www.tfhpublications.com

# Table of Contents

# Chapter 1

# Why I Adore My

# Pomeranian

Take a look at your tiny Pomeranian—can you imagine him pulling a sled through the icy Arctic Circle? Or herding an entire flock of sheep? Or guarding a village during the Stone Age? Well, believe it or not, ancestors of your furry little friend may have done just that! The Pomeranian (or "Pom" to his friends) is believed to be related to Spitz-type dogs who were found in many places in northern Europe and became particularly popular in Germany in the 1500s.

It was Queen Charlotte of England, a native of Germany, who brought these Spitz-type dogs to England in the 1700s. She called them "Pomeranians" because she obtained them from a region between eastern Germany and western Poland called Pomerania.

In the 1800s Queen Victoria, granddaughter of Charlotte, became interested in these dogs and established her own kennel for their breeding. Of course, the "Pomeranians" at that time were different than the little guys we know and love today—most of them weighed between 20 to 30 pounds (9 to 14 kg) and were much taller. It wasn't until Queen Victoria found a small 12-pound (5 kg) red sable Pom and began showing him with some success that the rage for the smaller type of dog began. The Queen also exhibited a dog named Gina, a lemon and white Pomeranian, who became a champion at London dog shows.

In 1870, when the breed was officially recognized, there were only three dogs entered at the first show in England. But thanks to the Queen, the popularity of these dogs rose steadily. In 1891, the first Pomeranian Club was formed, and by 1895 show entries rose to over 60. Five years later entries reached a total of 125.

Eventually the popularity of the breed

reached American shores. In 1888 the first Pomeranian (named Dick) was registered by the American Kennel Club (AKC). The Pomeranian was recognized as an official breed by the AKC in 1900.

## Characteristics of the Pomeranian

The Pomeranian is an adorable dog. He is willful, bold, and loyal—absolutely committed to his family; and he'll bring great joy to everyone in the home. Affectionate, small, a good protector, and a great friend, the Pomeranian is a fantastic breed for many types of people.

An advantage to owning a purebred dog is that it is much easier to predict how big he'll get, what type of coat he'll end up with, and what his personality will be like. Although it's important to remember that dogs are individuals, each breed does have its own distinct characteristics. These

*A larger version of today's Pomeranian was popular in Germany in the 1500s.*

characteristics can be found in the breed's standard—a written description of the dog that is used as a yardstick by breeders toward creating a "perfect" example of the breed and by which show judges compare animals.

So what does the "perfect" Pomeranian look and act like?

## Size

Pomeranians belong to the Toy Group of dog breeds. They are compact, active dogs.

Most Pomeranians weigh between 3 and 7 pounds (1.3 and 3.2 kg), and measure between 8 and 11 inches (20 and 28 cm) in height.

The Pomeranian's compact size is one of his most charming characteristics, but it can also be one of his most challenging. If left outside unsupervised, his small size allows him to crawl under fences or between fence posts.

## Head

Pomeranians have almost a fox-like appearance with darker hair around their noses and eyes and lighter hair through the remainder of their faces. Many will change their facial hair color as they grow older. The ears are high on the head and carried erect. Most Pomeranians have bright, almond-shaped brown eyes which accentuate their alert expressions and endearing glances. The head is usually carried high.

## FAMILY-FRIENDLY TIP
### Pomeranians and Children

Pomeranians are small and fragile, so they are best suited to homes with older, gentler children. Pomeranians are not recommended for homes with small children, as too much attention from active infants can make them nippy. Also, small children can at times be rough with animals— pulling hair or tugging on his ears. Pomeranians are proud little dogs who do not tolerate this type of behavior. Supervision is always necessary between any dog and a child; misunderstandings can happen even with the most well-behaved child or well-trained dog.

## Feet, Legs, and Gait

The shoulders and legs of the Pomeranian have more muscle than you might expect in a toy dog. Their legs and feet should be straight. Pomeranians are not inclined to stand on their hind legs unless begging for food.

The gait of the Pomeranian is smooth and balanced. Each rear leg moves in line with the front leg on the same side. Pomeranians are also fast. Without constant supervision outside, they can dash away without warning.

spend a few minutes petting him to revive his spirits, and make sure that he is not ill.

## Coat

His double coat consists of a soft, dense undercoat and a long, harsh-textured outer coat. His coat grows thickly around the neck and chest, which forms a ruff around his shoulders. This thick hair can be deceiving, making him appear much heavier than he actually is.

It takes time to groom his hair, but it is important to do so regularly. If grooming is neglected, the hair can tangle quite easily, so it is imperative to be vigilant about his grooming schedule. Most Pomeranians enjoy

8

My own Pom, Pierre, once escaped out the front door while I carried groceries inside. If you need to leave the outside door open for a prolonged period of time, it is a good idea to either gate them in another room or put a leash on them.

When excited, Pomeranians like to run in circles until they (and you) are exhausted. It can be fun to chase them around and change direction and make a game of this quirky behavior. It's also a great form of exercise for you both!

## Tail

The Pomeranian is famous for his tail. When he is happy, his tail sits comfortably on his back. When he is upset or not feeling well, his tail will hang down almost perpendicular to the floor. Therefore, his tail is often a predictor of what mood he is in at the time. If you do see his tail sagging,

## SENIOR DOG TIP

### When Is My Pom Considered a Senior?

One great advantage to a smaller breed like the Pomeranian is that they tend to live longer than larger breeds. A Pomeranian's life expectancy is about 15 years. Around age 7 your Pom would begin to be considered a senior.

being groomed, so it will be a pleasurable experience for both of you.

## Color

There are so many different color combinations of Pomeranians that no two look exactly alike. Your Pom may be black and tan, "brindle," which means a base color of gold or red with black cross stripes; be a solid red, orange, cream, or sable color; or have patches of white throughout the coat. As he ages, his hair color will continue to change (either darken or lighten up). My own Pierre started out sable in color, and as he's aged his coat has lightened considerably to an almost blonde hue.

## Temperament and Personality

Pomeranians are good at getting you to fall in love with them. One quick bat of those brown eyes, and you'll be sold! An intelligent breed, the Pomeranian exhibits a truly vivacious spirit that makes him the perfect companion dog.

Pomeranians are inquisitive and extroverted. While a Pom has a more independent streak than most other toy breeds, he still adores being involved in everything his owner is doing. Fiercely loyal, he responds enthusiastically to the sight of his

owner and is quite protective of him. He can get along with other dogs, especially other Pomeranians, but oftentimes he doesn't seem to understand his own size and may try to boss around or attack larger dogs. Pomeranians are inclined to chase cats and small animals, so careful introductions and supervision must be enforced when introducing a Pom to other family pets.

Pomeranians enjoy the pampered life—resting on soft, plush pillows and eating well are two of their favorite activities. Pomeranians do bark a lot, but females less frequently than their male counterparts. It is important to train your Pomeranian at a young age when and how often to bark (see Chapter 7 for more details).

While your Pom may look like a lap dog, he was used as a working dog in his past. He needs to run and play daily—a 15 minute walk twice a day is a good place to start. Weather permitting, a third time outside to play would help expel pent-up energy in your Pomeranian.

*Poms enjoy the pampered life—but don't forget to exercise them daily.*

# Chapter 2

# The Stuff of

# Everyday Life

Now that you have chosen to welcome a Pomeranian into your home, you need to purchase all the items which make everyday living more comfortable for you both. With so many products available to pet owners, it is hard to know where to begin, which items to buy, and how much of each item is necessary to have in the home. The large pet supply stores can be overwhelming with their jam-packed shelves and enticing displays. This chapter will help you decide which items are best suited for you and your Pomeranian.

## Bed

Pomeranians love to be pampered. Purchasing a bed just for him is one way to make him feel special. My Pom Pierre often slept on top of the pillows or curled up on top of bulky bedding, making a "nest" out of it, until I bought him a bed of his very own! There are a multitude of dog beds available—some can even be customized with your Pomeranian's name; some beds are even available heated.

If you are choosing a nest-style dog bed then select one that is approximately 16" x 21" (41 x 53 cm). If you want to buy a pillow bed then pick a pillow size of 30 to 36 inches (76 to 91 cm). Nest-styled beds are best for dogs who like to curl up, like your Pomeranian. Pillow beds are more suitable to dogs who like to sprawl out.

Make sure your bed is machine washable as you will want to launder it often to keep it clean and fresh for your Pomeranian.

## Carrier

There are many funky and functional carriers available to transport your Pomeranian. Most have removable, padded bottoms, elasticized safety collars, side mesh paneling for ventilation and viewing, as well as a zippered window so your Pomeranian can stick his head out to watch the world go by. There are front carriers available as well as tote, wheeled, and backpack varieties. Materials range from cotton and synthetics to leather. Price will usually dictate what material you eventually choose for his carrier. Select a bag that has been endorsed by the Humane Society and/or a national kennel club so you're sure you are buying a safe, quality carrier for your Pom. Shopping for the right carrier to match your Pomeranian's temperament can be a lot of fun—try them out together before you select one.

## Clothes

Clothes for small dogs have become very popular in recent years. Why dress up your Pomeranian? Small dogs often have very little body fat, so clothing can not only be fashionable, but also practical. Booties and sweaters for the winter months may help protect him from the cold. Even in the summer months, clothing can be important to protect a newly-shaven Pomeranian's skin from the sun's rays.

Make sure when choosing a piece of clothing for your Pomeranian that it fits well. You will want to ensure it doesn't hinder his vision, hearing, mobility, or breathing. Introduce clothing for short periods of time at first. If you start while your Pomeranian is a puppy he'll get used to it and learn to enjoy dressing up. There are many fashions to choose from—cotton is always a good choice because it breathes well and washes easily. Styles abound—just make sure there is nothing on the garment that could pose a choking hazard.

## Collar

Overall, flat buckle collars are the best choice for most dogs, including your Pomeranian. Puppies should wear only

## SENIOR DOG TIP

### Helping an Older Pomeranian Adapt to a New Home

Rescuing an older Pomeranian is a great way to find a loving family pet and help out a lonely dog in need. Of course, there will be an adjustment period for any new pet, but an older one in particular. In general, Pomeranians like routine and consistency—older ones like it even more. Keeping his bowl in the same spot each morning and feeding and walking him at the same time each day will help your older Pomeranian adapt to his new home.

buckle collars or harnesses. Buckle collars come in a variety of colors and are made with various materials like nylon and leather.

Nylon buckle collars are good for Pomeranians who exercise often or are in the water a lot. Nylon is very durable and washable, and also comes in a variety of colors. Many owners like to get matching collars and leashes.

Leather buckle collars wear well and are very long lasting. These collars start out rigid, or stiff, but will soften from the oils in your Pomeranian's skin over time.

Collars made of metal or chain are not a good idea for your tiny friend—they are far too heavy and can hurt his delicate neck. And, needless to say, any collar with prongs or that chokes your dog should never be used.

Fit is everything when it comes to collars. The collar should be tight enough that it won't slip off, but loose enough that you can fit two fingers between your Pom's neck and the collar.

## Crate

Instinctually, Pomeranians desire to have a den—a small, cozy place of their very own where they can feel safe and secure. A crate is just a modern version of a den. Crates not only give him a safe place to stay, but they can also make training your Pomeranian a lot easier. Housetraining goes much faster and smoother when you use a crate, and destructive chewing becomes easier to control. Traveling is safer too—for both you and your Pomeranian—when he's secured in a crate.

## What Type?

You can purchase a crate at your local pet store. The most popular crates are made of plastic or steel wire. Plastic crates are lightweight, portable, and are easily taken apart for storage or travel. Most plastic crates meet federal regulations for airline travel, if for some reason your Pomeranian can't fly in the cabin with you.

*Crates give your Pom a safe place to stay in the house.*

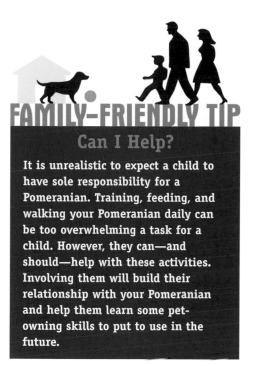

## Can I Help?

It is unrealistic to expect a child to have sole responsibility for a Pomeranian. Training, feeding, and walking your Pomeranian daily can be too overwhelming a task for a child. However, they can—and should—help with these activities. Involving them will build their relationship with your Pomeranian and help them learn some pet-owning skills to put to use in the future.

The quality of plastic crates can vary; you should choose one which is resistant to chewing.

Steel wire crates are also popular—the open design allows for more air flow than plastic crates. If your Pom is craving a more den-like place, you can place blankets over the wire crate to stem drafts and make the area dark.

When selecting the best crate for your Pomeranian, the American Veterinary Medical Association (AVMA) offers these guidelines:

- It should be large enough to allow the animal to stand (without touching the top of the cage), turn around, and lie down.

- It should be strong, with handles or grips and free of interior protrusions

- It should have a leak proof bottom that is covered with plenty of absorbent material.

- It should be purchased in advance so your dog can become acclimated to the crate prior to travel.

## Ex-Pen

Ex-pens provide your Pomeranian with a safe area to play in as an alternative to a crate. They allow for excellent ventilation and an open view of their surroundings. They are available in metal or washable materials. Most ex-pens have additional panels you can purchase to increase the play area for your Pomeranian. Ex-pens are easy to transport, set-up, take down, and store.

## Food and Water Bowls

Since your Pomeranian is a small dog his water and food bowls should be sized appropriately so he is comfortable eating and drinking. There are several different types of bowls: stainless steel, ceramic, plastic, and self-feeding.

Good
Dog

*Rubber on the bottom of a bowl can keep it from sliding.*

Use a stainless steel bowl if your Pomeranian is a nibbler. Stainless steel bowls are durable, long-lasting, easy to clean, and fairly inexpensive.

Ceramic bowls are good for Pomeranians who like to move their bowls around. Since ceramic is heavier than other materials used for feeding bowls, it's likely he'll be unable to move the bowl across the floor when eating. Because ceramic bowls are porous, it is essential that they be cleaned and sanitized daily. Replace cracked or chipped ceramic bowls immediately since they are likely to harbor bacteria in the cracks.

Plastic bowls are another alternative for your Pomeranian. They are the least expensive choice available and come in a variety of colors. You must be diligent about keeping plastic bowls clean, since they have a tendency to harbor bacteria.

Self feeders are good for the owner who is gone for most of the day or even overnight. These types of bowls are best for Pomeranians that are free-fed, meaning there is always food available to eat at any time.

All of your Pomeranian's dishes should be washed with hot soapy water daily or in the dishwasher to avoid the growth of bacteria. Having a second set of dishes can be helpful when the other is being cleaned.

## Food Storage

When considering bowls for your Pomeranian to eat and drink from, don't forget about a storage container for his food. Keeping the food in a canister with a lid extends the life of the food, reduces the breakdown of vitamins, and maintains freshness. Some manufacturers of dry food actually sell their product in a plastic container. If your Pomeranian eats canned food, using a can cover will help keep the moist food fresh.

## Gate

Gates can be very helpful for keeping your energetic and inquisitive Pomeranian from roaming about the house while you are gone. While Pomeranians tend to stay in a localized area when you are out, they will at times roam into the wrong

## Consistency!

From the start, consistency with your Pomeranian is important. You should feed and walk him close to the same time every day. Also, begin crate training as early as possible (with regular breaks for feeding, walking, and playtime, of course.)

door and the width of the doorway. Extra wide gates are available. There are also hands-free gates which open when you step on a pedal and elaborate gates that open and close at the touch of a button.

## Grooming Supplies

Grooming is essential for a breed like the Pomeranian. There are many grooming supplies available on the market, and it's important to purchase ones specifically suited for your dog to ensure he is groomed properly. Grooming is a great bonding opportunity and should be a pleasurable experience for you both. It is important to keep that in mind when choosing your supplies.

Here are the basic items you'll need:

• **Brushes**: A soft wire slicker brush is good for your Pomeranian's body. A pure bristle brush or pin brush is excellent for his mane.

• **Comb**: Avoid cheap plastic combs; use the good steel ones—they glide through the hair easily and break less coat. Combs should have rounded teeth at least 3/4 in to 1 inch (2 to 2.5 cm) long.

• **Scissors:** A pair of 6 inch (15 cm) straight edge scissors made for dogs is a good basic scissor.

• **Nail clippers:** There are several varieties of nail clippers on the

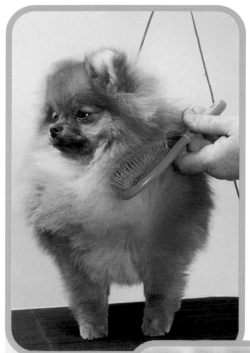

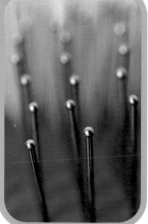

*The pins on a pin brush can help tame your Pom's mane.*

room. I once returned home from work to discover that my Pomeranian Pierre ventured down to the basement. That was a good indication that a gate was necessary.

When purchasing a gate you will want to keep in mind the height of the market, including guillotine and scissor type. I find clippers made for babies a good choice for a small dog.

- **Shampoo and conditioner:** You'll want a shampoo that cleans but doesn't dry your Pom's skin and a conditioner that doesn't leave the hair limp. Avoid products with harsh chemicals and additives. Ask your breeder or vet for suggestions. Experiment until you find products you like.

- **Spray bottle;** A spray bottle is useful for misting your Pom's hair with diluted conditioner. This will help soften his coat and make brushing a more tolerable experience for you both.

- **Small-size dog toothbrush:** or Finger Brush and Dog Toothpaste: Don't forget dental care for your dog! Many people find finger brushes much easier to work with than toothbrushes, and my own Pom loves his liver-flavored toothpaste.

## ID Tags

ID tags are available on-line or through any pet store. Remember to include all pertinent information including the name of your Pomeranian, your address, and a home or cell phone number where you can be reached. Keep the tags on your Pom's collar at all times—it's the best way to help ensure his swift return if he's ever lost.

## Microchipping

Another form of identification available for your Pomeranian is a microchip. It's a tiny metal transponder approximately the size of a grain of rice. The chip carries a unique identification number and is implanted under your Pomeranian's skin (usually between the shoulder blades; behind the neck area). These microchips are registered with local and/or national databases and shelters. Most shelters and veterinarian offices have scanners to read the chips. Once read, the staff can call a 24 hour hotline to get your contact information. Your veterinarian can implant the chip in a painless procedure.

## Leash

At the same time you purchase a collar, you should purchase a narrow, six-foot (2 m) leather, cotton, or nylon leash.

Nylon leashes are very durable and washable and come in a variety of colors. Leather leashes, like their collar counterparts, are very sturdy and long lasting. And like collars, the leather leash will soften over time from the oils in your skin, making it more comfortable to hold.

Cotton webbed leashes are another alternative. These are washable, easy on the hands, and inexpensive. They are available in a variety of lengths. The 20-foot (6 m) length, known as a "long line," is ideal to use when teaching your Pomeranian to come when called. This allows him the freedom to roam a distance away from you while you are still maintaining control.

Retractable leashes are another alternative for your Pomeranian. A unique feature about a retractable leash is the ability to control how little or how much lead he is given. The nylon lead is rolled up and housed within a plastic casing that you hold in your hand. A spring-type function allows the lead to automatically lengthen or shorten (retract) as the dog travels. A one-button braking system stops him from traveling any farther. It also serves as a locking mechanism should you want to keep him at a consistent distance. You'll still need to keep an eye on him while he's on this type of lead, but you and your dog might love the flexibility of a retractable leash.

## Harness

A harness is a great alternative to a leash attached to a collar, especially for a small dog like your Pom, who has a very delicate neck. Harnesses are available in various materials including nylon and leather. If the harness is for walking your Pomeranian, a padded

## Licensing Your Pomeranian

You should investigate your local animal control laws to make sure your Pomeranian meets current licensing requirements. Usually this just requires an application fee and regular rabies vaccinations.

one is the best choice. If the harness is for use in the car, buy one specifically made for that function so you're sure he will be safe while traveling. Also ensure the one you are choosing is made specifically for a small dog so that it will secure your Pomeranian properly.

## Toys

As you've probably discovered by now, Pomeranians seem to have an abundance of energy. Playing with toys is a great way to help them expend some extra energy, so it is important to select items they will love as much as you do.

An old t-shirt, pillowcase, towel, or blanket, can be very comforting to your

## Doggy Daycare

Doggy daycares are becoming more and more popular each passing year. Similar to a child's daycare, you drop off and pick up your Pomeranian during designated hours. Trained staff keep your Pomeranian busy with indoor and outdoor activities. You must present proof of current vaccinations if you choose to enroll your Pomeranian.

Some important questions to ask when choosing the right daycare for your Pomeranian are:

- Does the play space seem adequate for him?
- What about the resting space?
- Are larger and smaller dogs separated?
- Is the perimeter of the facility secure?
- Is the center clean and odor-free?
- Are the toys size-appropriate and cleaned often?
- Is the staff knowledgeable about dogs?
- Is there an adequate human to dog ratio (at least one person for every 10 dogs)?
- Is there a plan for emergencies (who to call if something is wrong with your Pomeranian)?

Pomeranian, especially if the item smells like you. Be forewarned that this item is likely to be destroyed. Be reticent of giving your Pomeranian an old pair of shoes to play with, since he won't be able to distinguish between an old pair and a new pair. Providing your Pomeranian with his own toys will keep him away from your shoes and other items that you wouldn't want him to destroy.

Remember that your Pomeranian is small so purchase size-appropriate toys—ones that will fit easily in his mouth and aren't too heavy for him to carry. Plush toys shaped like fun characters, rubber toy bones, toys that can be stuffed with food, balls, rope toys—the sky's the limit for items made especially for small dogs.

Some owners give their dogs toys made for children. Keep in mind that when giving your Pomeranian a toy that was not made for a dog, you must check the label and make sure it doesn't say "not for children under three." This is usually a warning that the insides of the toy may contain harmful material or small pieces may break off and become a choking hazard.

Don't just buy toys and expect your dog to amuse himself. Many of your Pomeranian's toys should be interactive (even if it's just the two of you playing with a rubber ball). Interactive play is very important for your Pom because he needs active people time. Playing with toys allows your Pomeranian to expel built-up energy and reduces

*Make sure your Pom's toys are safe and size-appropriate.*

stress related to confinement. Play also offers an opportunity for socialization and helps him learn appropriate and inappropriate behavior.

Keep your Pomeranian entertained by rotating his toys. Put old toys out of sight for a month or two and then bring them out again—he will enjoy them just as much as when they were new. In our home we use a basket to house Pierre's toys. When he is tired of playing with items set out for him on the floor, he will reach into the basket, and with his mouth, pull a new toy out.

## Keeping Your Pom Entertained

Pomeranians are active, intelligent dogs who need both mental and physical stimulation. Here are some tips to keeping them happy:

- If you think your dog might be lonely when you aren't home, try leaving the radio or television on while your are gone—the noise will keep him company.
- Take him with you! Include him on family outings. Take him to the park, to the beach, or to a dog-friendly neighbor's house. Your dog will love being out and about with you.
- Pomeranians love to be petted. There are even "doggy massage" techniques you can find out about online or in books. Petting and stroking your dog is not only beneficial to his metal health, but also recent studies have shown that this kind of contact is a great stress reducer for humans.

The Stuff of Everyday Life

# Chapter 3

# Good Eating

What we feed our dogs has evolved quite a bit over the years. In the past, "canine nutrition" was not a concept many people considered. Recently, however, what constitutes a balanced and healthy diet for dogs has been the topic of much research and debate. Luckily for our furry friends, this interest in nutrition has positively affected the quality of commercial food and spurred a growth of alternative doggy diets.

Consulting your veterinarian about the best diet for your Pomeranian is a great place to start. Your vet will point you in the right direction and help you decipher what is the right food for him among the multitude of choices available. Remember to re-visit this discussion with your veterinarian every few years.

Your small dog needs the same type of nutrition as a larger dog—he just doesn't eat quite as much. Pomeranians do love food, though, and most will eat just about anything you give them. That's why it's up to you to pick out something nutritious.

Your Pomeranian needs a combination of fats, carbohydrates, proteins, vitamins, minerals, and water in his diet. Mary L. Wulff-Tilford, author of *All You Ever Wanted to Know about Herbs for Pets*, says, "The food your animal eats should provide all of the nutritional components which are necessary for all organs and systems of a healthy body to perform in harmonious unison. A properly functioning body does an amazing job at preventing disease and healing itself, and to do this it requires the energies and nutrients of a well-balanced diet."

Before discussing the different types of food available to feed your Pom, there's one other essential element to his diet you'll need to remember—water. Have plenty of fresh water available to your Pomeranian at all times.

## Dinner Time Tip

Feeding your dog at the same time every day is a good idea—dogs like consistency. When setting his dinner time, keep in mind that your Pomeranian may not be able to withstand sleeping the entire night without having to be walked after eating his dinner. You may want to give him his evening meal early so you have sufficient time to walk him.

## Commercial Foods

Commercial pet food is a great convenience for busy pet owners and those who are not inclined to make their own (see section on Non-Commercial Diets, below). The first commercially prepared pet food was a dog biscuit introduced in England around 1860. Since then, semi-moist, canned, and dry foods have been introduced.

The pet food industry is huge and extremely profitable. Although it is not necessary to buy the most expensive food on the market, this is a case where cheaper is not better. Low-cost foods tend to use inexpensive ingredients so the company can save some money on the cost of making the food. Cheaper ingredients and an excess of fillers might end up short-changing your Pomeranian on his diet.

## Reading the Label

So how do you pick a good commercial food? Learn how to read the label. The first thing you should look for is the "AAFCO guarantee"—this is the approval from the Association of American Feed Control Officials (AFFCO) given to commercial foods that meet their standards. These standards were formulated in the early 1990s by panels of pet nutrition experts. A food may be certified in two ways: (1) by meeting AAFCO's published standards for content ("Nutrient Profiles"), or (2) by passing

## FAMILY-FRIENDLY TIP

### Can Your Child Help Feed Your Pomeranian?

Helping feed the family Pomeranian can be a great chore for an older child. Putting a measured amount of food in a bowl and then placing it on the dog's mat can be a rewarding lesson in responsibility. Keep in mind that you will need to supervise—never just assume the job has been done. Also, if you allow children to give your Pomeranian treats, be sure the treat is held in the palm of your child's open hand, and not grasped in the fingers. This makes it easier for the dog to take it and less of a potentially anxious situation for the child if your Pomeranian tries too aggressively to retrieve the treat.

feeding tests or trials. Keep in mind that the standards set only "minimums" and "maximums," not "optimums." Commercial foods are designed to be adequate for the average animal, but not all foods will be suitable for your particular Pomeranian's needs.

The next thing on the label you'll want to inspect is the ingredients. It is very important to read the ingredient list before purchasing any type of food

*Kibble is the most popular form of commercial dog food.*

for your Pomeranian. The first ingredient listed should be a whole meat or fish, not a by-product, "meal," or water. The specific name of the meat should be listed ("beef") not a general term like "poultry" or "meat," because in that case you have no idea what the source of the meat is. Try to avoid artificial colors, flavors, and sweeteners—they haven't been proven to be dangerous to your Pom, but they're not good for him, either. Also, look for a food with natural preservatives like vitamins C and E (tocopherols), not artificial preservatives like propyl gallate, BHA, or ethoxyquin.

Pet food labels often carry words like "dinner," "entrée," and "flavor." What appears on the label is regulated by the Food and Drug Administrations (FDA), and here's a crash course in what they mean:

- **The 95% rule.** If the product says "Beef Dog Food," 95% of the product must be the named ingredients. A product with a combination label, such as "Beef and Liver for Dogs," must contain 95% beef and liver, and there must be more beef than liver, since beef is named first. This applies primarily to canned foods containing meat, poultry and fish.

- **The 25% or "dinner" rule.** Ingredients named on the label must comprise at least 25% of the product but less than 95%, when there is a qualifying term like "dinner," "entree," "formula," "platter," "nuggets," etc. In "Beef Dinner for Dogs," beef may or may not be the primary ingredient. If two ingredients are named ("Beef and Turkey Dinner for Dogs"), the two ingredients must total 25%, there must be more of the first ingredient (beef) than the second (turkey), and there must be at least 3% of the lesser ingredient.

- **The 3% or "with" rule.** A product may be labeled "Dog Food with Beef" if it contains at least 3% of the named ingredient. This is tricky— you must pay close attention to whether you're purchasing "Beef Dog Food" (95% beef) or "Dog Food with Beef" (3% beef).

- **The "flavor" rule.** A food may be labeled "Turkey Flavor Dog Food" even if the food does not contain turkey, as long as there is a "sufficiently detectable" amount of flavor. This may be derived from meals, broths, by-products, or "digests" of various parts from the animal species indicated on the label.

Some commercial pet food ingredients can cause problems like allergies, food intolerance, inflammatory bowel disease, and other illnesses. Therefore, it is important to monitor your Pomeranian for any problems if you introduce a new commercial food to his diet.

## Commercial Food "Dos and Dont's"

Here are some tips to consider when selecting your Pomeranian's food:

- When selecting food, make sure the label has an "AAFCO guarantee."
- Don't buy a food containing "by-product meal" or "meat and bone

## How to Read a Food Label

There are two sections of written material on your Pomeranian's food packaging: the principal display panel and the information panel. Included on the principal display is the brand name, the description of the food ("Chicken and rice in gravy), what class and category of food (growth/puppy) and finally the quantity. The information panel includes the ingredient list, the nutritional value, and feeding instructions.

meal." The contents and quality of these "meals" can vary tremendously and are not a reliable source of nutrition for your Pomeranian.

- Avoid foods that rely on by-products as the sole source of protein. By-products consist of organs and other parts either not desired, or condemned, for human consumption.

- Look for a named meat as the first ingredient.

- Avoid generic or store brands. They generally contain cheaper and poorer quality ingredients.

- Unless specifically recommended by your veterinarian, avoid "light," "senior," or "special formula," foods.

*A high-quality food will help keep your Pomeranian looking and feeling good.*

the moist variety), and the hard texture reduces tarter build-up on your Pomeranian's teeth. Pomeranians are prone to early tooth loss, so feeding them dry food is highly recommended to keep their teeth and gums in good condition.

Common ingredients found in kibble include rice flour, ground corn, and lamb or chicken meal. There are quite a few brands to choose from so it's important to read the ingredients list carefully and consult with your veterinarian to ensure you select the best one for your Pomeranian. Remember that the dry food can get stale and lose some of its nutritional value so check the expiration date and make sure you replace it fairly often. You should also store kibble in a cool, dry place, preferably in an airtight container.

If you decide to feed dry food, don't be alarmed if you find kibble bits strewn about the house. Pomeranians enjoy taking small bites of food from their bowl and carrying them a distance away to eat them.

These foods may contain excessive fiber and/or inadequate fats that can result in skin, coat, and other health concerns.

- Select brands preserved naturally. Many brands are now preserved with vitamins C and E instead of chemicals.

- Check the expiration date to ensure freshness.

### Types of Commercial Food

Your Pomeranian should do well on any of several dry or canned dog foods, depending on his level of activity, metabolism, and individual body chemistry.

### Dry Food

Dry food (also called "kibble,") is the most popular type of commercial dog food. It is inexpensive (compared to

### Canned Food

Canned foods contain as much as 75 percent water and can include color enhancers such as iron oxide and sodium nitrate. While finicky dogs may prefer the taste of canned food over dry, most experts consider it a poor

choice for a total diet—dry foods are considered better because they are nutritionally denser than canned, and therefore your dog needs less of it for a complete diet. Many owners do include a scoop of canned mixed in with dry kibble, just to give their Poms a little extra flavor and moisture.

There are companies that offer canned food with no by-products, no artificial flavors, no wheat, no artificial preservatives, no corn, no white rice, and no artificial colors. At one time these types of food were hard to find, but more and more pet stores and pet superstores are carrying them. Check labels and ingredients to compare these alternatives to mainstream canned food manufacturers.

### Semi-moist Food

Semi-moist foods are cooked combinations of soybean meal, sugar, fresh meat or meat by-products, animal fat, preservatives, and humectants (wetting agents that allow the product to stay moist but not spoil). Although most dogs love the taste of semi-moist food, they are typically full of sugar and preservatives and will do nothing to help your dog's teeth. Always keep your Pomeranian's health (as well as his taste buds) in mind when making a food selection.

## What About Organic Foods?

Organic pet food sales are growing at nearly three times the rate of human organic food sales, says the Organic Trade Association. Still, organic pet foods remain a tiny fraction (0.09%) of total pet food sales, but for those committed to an organic lifestyle, this type of food is an excellent choice. Organic pet foods, much like their human counterparts, do tend to cost a bit more than non-organic food. Organic food does have proponents among holistic veterinarians, but many traditional veterinarians concur that there's no proof that organic pet food, at any price, can assure a pet of a longer or better life. As always, you should check with your veterinarian before switching to organic food to make certain it contains a balanced diet for your Pomeranian.

## Non-Commercial Diets

Some people choose a different route when feeding their dog. There are non-commercial options, like raw food or home cooking, which are growing in

29

Good Eating

popularity with dog owners. While these alternative diets may take more time than picking up prepared food from a pet store, they give dog owners much more control over what goes into their dog's diet.

### Home-Cooked Diet

Commercial dog food is convenient and easy, but does not offer equal quality. Less expensive brands may have too many calories and too few vitamins, minerals, proteins, or carbohydrates, and premium brands may be too high or low in protein, calories, and other nutrients. Therefore, if you have the time and culinary skills necessary, making your own food can be a healthy and cost-effective alternative. The meals need not be complicated. Protein and a vegetable mixed together would be a sufficient dinner for your Pomeranian.

Before starting on a home-cooked diet plan,

## Supplements

If you are feeding your Pomeranian a balanced diet, there should be no need for supplementation. If your veterinarian does suggest supplements, many organic and natural food manufacturers offer them. You can find them online or at a natural food store.

talk to your vet and do your research. There are several books and websites dedicated to providing healthy recipes for your canine companion. You will need to figure out what is (and what is not) okay to feed your Pomeranian. For instance, your home-cooked meals need to have the right balance of omega-3 and omega-6 fatty acids for joint and skin health.

### Raw Diet

Raw food diets, also called BARF (bones and raw food) diets, have gained popularity in the last few years. This diet consists of freshly ground raw meat and bones, ground vegetables and fruit, and sometimes cooked grains as well. The diet is modeled after what dogs ate in the wild, before they became domesticated.

*Home-cooked diets are growing in popularity.*

If you feed a raw diet, like a home-cooked diet you must be sure it is nutritionally balanced. You cannot just throw raw meat into your Pomeranian's bowl and expect him to thrive. Research and a discussion with your vet are necessary before you embark on a raw diet for your dog.

Proponents of the raw diet claim dogs thrive on this food plan, and it can even help dogs with chronic conditions like allergies. Raw chicken and turkey necks are a great way to clean teeth, provide natural calcium and phosphorus, and add variety to your Pomeranian's diet. Just keep in mind you should never give your dog a cooked bone—these easily splinter and can cause internal damage.

The raw diet is not without its controversy. Many vets do not believe the meat source is safe enough to feed raw, and there is potential for food-borne illnesses. If you are feeding your Pomeranian raw meat, be sure to wash your hands thoroughly after handling. Thaw meat in the refrigerator, not on the countertop. Warm water can be used to thaw or warm the food after it has been mostly thawed in the refrigerator.

One other drawback to raw food diets is that they take more time to prepare than commercial ones. That's why some commercial producers have come up with frozen raw foods that contain raw meat, grains, and fresh vegetables designed to provide complete nutrition. They can be found online and in natural food stores.

## Introducing a New Food

Anytime you decide to change your Pomeranian's diet, you should first talk you your veterinarian. A sudden change in your Pom's food, like from commercial kibble to a raw diet, may

31

### What if Your Pomeranian Is Choking?

1. Open his mouth and look for the blockage. If you can see or feel anything, remove it.
2. If you can't see the blockage, lay him on his side on the floor. Place a pillow under his hips so his head is lower than his hindquarters.
3. Place both hand on his diaphragm (just beneath the rib cage) and rapidly depress four or five times in a thrusting motion.
4. Get him to your vet immediately.

*Puppies have different nutritional demands than adults.*

give him diarrhea, constipation, or both as his system adjusts to the new food. You'll need to go slowly and feed him small amounts of the new food at first.

If you are changing brands of commercial food, start by mixing 1/4 of the new food with 3/4 of the old food. Then gradually increase it to half and half, and then over a few weeks totally replace the old food with the new. This method can also work if you are changing diets.

When introducing a new food, watch for changes in your Pomeranian's skin and coat, appetite, energy level, mood, itchiness, discharges or odors, body weight, and the size and consistency of stool.

## Age-Appropriate Feeding

Puppies have different nutritional demands for their growing bodies than adults. Puppies need about twice the amount of calories as an adult. Pomeranian puppies should be fed specially formulated puppy food to help build bones and muscles. Until they are about six months old, they should be fed three or four times a day. After six months, you can reduce that amount to two feedings.

At about one year, Pomeranians are considered an adult, although it can vary by individual. Talk to your vet about switching to an adult food when your Pom is nearing a year old.

Most dogs are considered seniors around age seven, but toy dogs tend to live longer than larger dogs, and your Pom's senior years might be closer to 10. Most Pomeranian owners don't find a need to switch to a different dog food for their older dog if he is in good health. Issues like obesity, diabetes, or kidney disease that can affect older dogs may merit a change in his diet—your vet will advise you in cases like this.

## When Should I Feed My Pom?

You not only have a myriad of choices for what to feed your Pomeranian, you'll also have to decide when to feed him. Some owners choose to schedule feedings at a certain time during the day, and take away any uneaten food after a period of time. Other people choose to "free-feed," which means food is constantly available and your Pomeranian eats when he is hungry. Scheduled feedings usually take place in the morning and evening and consist of similar amounts of food at each feeding. Pomeranians who follow a scheduled feeding routine are often easier to train since the scheduled feedings can serve as a reward for good behavior.

While free feeding is the easiest method, it is not recommend for multiple dog households, since one dog may stop eating (a sign of illness) and you will not be able to tell. Also, leaving food out all day can encourage your dog to eat more, and he may end up with an obesity problem. Also, if your Pomeranian spends many hours

alone, free feeding may not be ideal since he will need to eliminate what he has consumed.

## Treat Tips

Try not to feed your Pomeranian food or snacks in between meals. It can be challenging to withstand the begging of your adorable Pomeranian, but it is in his best interest to not feed him

## SENIOR DOG TIP

### Feeding the Older Pomeranian

Special, "light" diets are available for older dogs, which consist of a reduced amount of protein. While you will want to watch your older Pom's weight, Dr. Franco suggests in an article in *Veterinary Forum*, "Benefits from a reduced protein diet typical of existing canine geriatric products have never been proven, and the possibility exists that reduced protein diets are not in the best interest of the geriatric patient." As long as your older Pom doesn't have any weight or health problems, it's a good idea to keep feeding him his regular diet.

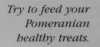

*Try to feed your Pomeranian healthy treats.*

table food. If you do give him treats or table food between meals, you are forming a bad habit, and he will now expect you to feed him anytime food is present. If you do not want an overweight Pomeranian or one who is constantly begging you and your guests for food then it is vital to avoid feeding him table scraps.

Choosing a healthy treat is important. Avoid items with sugar, artificial colors, flavors or preservatives. Look for treats that include meat and whole grains. Marrow bones, raw carrots, boiled liver, chicken or beef cubes are all great choices for your Pomeranian.

## Food No-No's

Don't give these items to your Pom—many are not only unhealthy, but can be dangerous.

- Chocolate contains theobromine, a chemical that is toxic to dogs.
- Certain mushrooms are dangerous and can produce abdominal pain, liver and kidney damage, and anemia.
- Excessive garlic can causing vomiting, liver damage, anemia, and diarrhea.
- Onions can cause haemolytic anaemia.
- Bones that can splinter or that have sharp edges.
- Macadamia nuts contain an unknown toxin that causes tremors and paralysis.
- Food with caffeine, including coffee and tea
- Raisins and grapes
- Moldy or spoiled food
- Alcohol

## Obesity

Obesity in dogs is a serious medical problem. Overweight Pomeranians are more prone to injury, have more stress on their heart, lungs, liver, kidneys, and joints, and can experience problems in surgery. Also, keep in mind that orthopedic problems are often caused by obesity.

How can you tell if your Pomeranian is overweight? If he becomes slow and his movements are cumbersome, that is a good indication he may be carrying too many pounds. Also, if he has difficulty chasing a ball and he becomes more obsessive about food, those are indicators too. Feel his body—his rib should be discernable, but not prominent. Consult with your veterinarian if you think your dog has a problem. He or she can weigh your dog on a scale to get his exact poundage. A healthy Pomeranian should weigh about seven pounds (3.2 kg) or less.

A healthy diet and exercise are the best ways to keep your Pom from becoming obese. It is critical to provide your Pomeranian with exercise every day and some opportunity for prolonged exercise a couple of times a week. Long walks, play sessions, and

*Exercise and a healthy diet will help keep your Pom's weight under control.*

training sessions help keep muscles in shape. Time alone in a yard is not sufficient, as he more than likely won't exercise on his own. Two dogs, however, will usually play together and can exercise each other, but you'll still want to go for a daily walk.

You control your Pom's diet, so cut down on treats, or substitute high-calorie snacks with pieces of carrot. Don't just put your dog on a crash diet—talk to your vet about how much and what food is healthy for your dog. Other tips to help keep your Pomeranian's weight in check: keep him away from the table at mealtime, separate him from snacking children, and don't let anyone, including your kids, feed him without supervision.

## Table Manners for Your Pomeranian

It is important to teach proper table manners to your Pomeranian very early so there is no or little opportunity for poor behavior to begin. One table scrap can lead to a life-time of table-side begging. Refrain from feeding him your dinner from the start—he'll be healthier, and you'll be happier in the end.

# Chapter 4

# Looking Good

With their fluffy coats and proud tails, Pomeranians can make anyone coo over them —they are truly adorable dogs. To keep them looking their best and brightest, regular grooming will need to be a priority in your home. A Pomeranian does not require as much grooming as some of the other long haired breeds, but do be prepared to brush him at least two or three times weekly. The occasional bath, weekly nail trim, eye, ear, and dental care round out the grooming process.

Grooming provides great bonding time for you and your Pomeranian. Speaking to him in a quiet and calm voice while brushing him will allow the experience to be a relaxing one for both of you. But more than this, it is good for his health! This one on one time allows you to check his body for lumps and bumps, and notice any changes to his skin. Include an examination of your Pomeranian's feet into a grooming session to make sure there is nothing stuck between his pads. Check your Pomeranian thoroughly to make sure he has no cuts, sores, fleas, rashes, ticks, or dirt in his ears.

## Start Grooming Early

You should introduce regular grooming to your Pomeranian while he is still a puppy. He will learn to enjoy it and expect it as a routine experience if done so at an early age. And if you've adopted an older Pom, it's never too late to start—you'll just need to go slowly and have plenty of patience with him. Make sure you choose a grooming time when your Pomeranian is calm and you have adequate time to spend on the endeavor. And never underestimate the power of praise—be sure to praise him often while grooming. This will help make grooming a pleasurable experience for both you and your dog.

## Coat and Skin Care

Your Pomeranian has an abundant, stand-off double coat, consisting of a soft cottony undercoat and a topcoat of harsher guard hairs. Because of his thick coat you will need to work gently with him. His double-coat can make grooming a challenge, but keeping it neat and trim will make you both feel better.

Your Pomeranian will go through various changes in his or her coat during the years. At about three months a Pomeranian puppy loses that cloud-soft puppy fluff, and for several months what was a cute little puff ball can start to look a bit ragged. Don't worry—this is normal. Your Pom's adult coat starts to appear at about a year old.

## Grooming Supplies

- Pin brush
- Metal comb
- Slicker brush
- Scissors
- Spray bottle
- Coat conditioner
- Pet shampoo/conditioner
- Blow dryer
- Towels
- Nail clippers
- Styptic powder
- Dog toothpaste and toothbrush or fingerbrush
- Cotton balls
- Mineral oil
- Grooming table (optional)

*Use a pin brush to keep your Pomeranian's coat groomed.*

your Pom will certainly mat. Extremely matted dogs end up having their coats shaved, which eliminates the very benefits of this breed's coat—protection from both cold and heat.

You'll need a pin brush, a metal comb, a slicker brush (for removing mats), a spray bottle, and some coat conditioner. Invest in the highest-quality tools you can afford—they might be a bit more expensive, but will last a long time.

Your Pomeranian needs his coat brushed weekly. Don't brush him dry—spray his coat with coat conditioner, or even water from a spray bottle. Adding a little conditioner will make the process a bit easier on both of you as it softens his hair and enables the brush to move more smoothly through his coat.

## How?

Using a pin brush, start from the top of the shoulder, parting his coat and brushing the hair to the right or left of the coat. This method is called "line brushing." Spray the part with more conditioner or water, and brush from the skin out to the end of the hair— just be gentle and careful not to scrape the skin. Continue down the part and when you reach the end, return to the top and make another part to the right of the first part. Then repeat the

The good news for owners of a male Pomeranian is once he is about 18 months of age his coat will stay relatively the same year in year out. With an intact Pomeranian female you will not be so lucky, as the hormonal changes with seasons often wreak havoc on her coat. Whelping and rearing a litter usually result in a complete shed—it will take her at least six months to re-grow her coat after a litter. This is a great reason to have your Pom neutered if you haven't already done so.

## Brushing

Brushing stimulates circulation and gives your Pomeranian a shinier coat. Routine brushing and combing also remove dead hair and prevent matting. Mats are extremely painful to your dog, and if you neglect his brushing routine process: Part—brush—mist. Then brush his chest and tail, then around his legs to finish up.

If you encounter any mats on the way, try to untangle them with a fine-toothed comb or slicker brush. If the mats are particularly stubborn, you can cut them out with a pair of scissors, and remind yourself to brush your Pom a little more often to prevent those mats! Remember to take your time and be gentle. I will often place my hand at the root of Pierre's hair to limit the discomfort he feels when his knotted ends are being combed.

If your Pomeranian has gotten into any sticky or gooey substances like tar or gum don't use commercial solvents or industrial cleaners on his coat. Many of these are toxic. Try dissolving the substances with mineral oil. If you're unable to remove them, carefully clip away the affected areas.

## Trimming

When trimming your Pomeranian's fur with scissors, always cut in the direction the hair is growing (scissors should be parallel to the growth of the fur). Always cut his fur with the pointed end of the scissors away from his sensitive areas as sudden, jerky movements can cause injury to your Pomeranian.

*Pomeranians need to be brushed at least once a week.*

## The Shed

Any Pomeranian owner will tell you—this breed is a constant shedder, so be prepared. Pomeranian hair grows and dies just as human hair does. The cottony undercoat sheds once or twice a year, and care must be given to the Pomeranian's coat especially during his semi-annual shedding periods. Shedding can take anywhere from three weeks to two months. A warm bath helps accelerate the process, and daily (or twice-daily) grooming can help control clouds of hair that scurry into corners and under furniture.

## Bathing

What could be more fun than bathing your Pomeranian? Most Pomeranians don't mind getting wet and will remain calm during the process. Too-frequent baths can dry the natural oils in his skin and lead to constant scratching, which in turn can lead to bacterial infections. Therefore, do not bathe him too often. Once a month is a good schedule to keep. If necessary, you can rinse his hindquarters to maintain cleanliness.

Gather all of your supplies before

you plunge your Pom into the water—the last thing you want is to be searching the house for a dry towel with a dripping wet dog under your arm! You'll need: a pin brush, shampoo, conditioner, a towel, and a hair dryer. Why the pin brush? To prevent mats, you must brush your Pom before you bathe him. Otherwise, he'll be one little wet matted mess!

There are many different types of pet shampoo on the market—each formulated for problems such as dry itchy skin, inflamed or scaling skin, fleas and ticks, doggy odor, skunk odor, abnormal shedding, quick rinsing for dogs that don't like to take a bath, and coat shine to bring out the natural luster of your dog's coat. There are organic and natural ones available, too. You may want to try a hypoallergenic shampoo/conditioner that will gently clean and condition your Pomeranian's coat in one step. It would be a good idea to consult with your veterinarian before using any of these products on your dog.

*Many people find it easy to bathe their small dogs in the sink.*

## Where?

Where should you bathe your Pom? In warm weather, I find it a nice treat to bathe my Pomeranian outside. Choose a place that will not turn to mud when it gets wet. It's a good idea a have a washtub large enough for your Pomeranian to stand up in and fill it with a few inches of water. Water straight from a garden hose may start off warm, but usually gets too cold quickly. You can alleviate this problem by purchasing a water temperature mixer valve assembly that can connect to your water source and will help

## Do I Need a Grooming Table?

Grooming tables have arms and a break-away noose that keep your Pom in place when he's being groomed. Professional groomers use them, and so do people who show their dogs. Some people find them very useful in the home, but since they are costly and can take time setting up and dismantling, it is not a necessary piece of equipment for grooming your Pomeranian.

keep his water warm. Most valve assemblies hook up to your existing washing machine water supply. When it's time for his bath, just connect a hose to the valve assembly and run it outside.

If the weather doesn't agree, or if you'd rather bathe your Pomeranian inside, the sink is a good choice. You won't have to worry about regulating the water temperature and you may find it easier on your back to bathe him in a sink instead of the tub. Just remember to put down a non-skid mat at the bottom to prevent your Pom from slipping and hurting himself.

Another alternative is to purchase a raised dog bath. An ergonomically designed dog grooming bathing tub elevates your dog to a level that is comfortable for you and keeps your Pomeranian securely contained. This bath can help your Pomeranian not slip or slide when being bathed as it comes with a padded non-slip surface. If you want to spend the extra money, raised dog baths are available in most pet shops and online stores.

### How?

So are you ready to give your Pom a bath? Wait! You've thoroughly brushed his coat to prevent matting, right? Okay, now you can begin.

It's a good idea to let your Pomeranian get used to the sound of the running water. This will help him stay at ease during the bath. Fill the sink or tub with a few inches of warm water, and check the temperature to make sure it's not too hot or too cool. Then put him into the bath. Starting from his head thoroughly wet your Pomeranian with warm water. It can be helpful to use a plastic pitcher or a spray nozzle attached to the faucet. Never spray water directly onto your dog's face or genitals, and avoid getting water into his ears. Some owners place cotton balls in the ears to prevent water from getting in.

Put a small bit of shampoo in your hand, and work it into your dog's coat starting at his neck and working your way toward the tail. Then rinse him thoroughly with warm water. Shampoo residue can cause skin irritations so make sure you give your Pomeranian's coat a thorough rinsing.

Towel drying him in the bath will remove some of the excess water before you take him out of the tub. If you want to get your Pomeranian dry faster specialty pet-drying towels are available at various pet stores. Some will absorb 10 times their own weight in water!

Don't let your Pom's coat dry naturally—a damp undercoat can cause skin problems and will be more likely to mat. Use your pin brush to gently brush him dry, with the hair dryer on the lowest setting, being very careful it never gets hot enough to burn your dog's skin. This allows the coat to dry completely and avoid the spatter of water if he runs about the house shaking his wet coat.

## FAMILY-FRIENDLY TIP
### "Can I Help?"

Your child may watch the grooming routine of the family dog and want to help out. While it is probably best that an adult take on the grooming responsibility of your Pomeranian, your child certainly can learn to help out. He or she can help gather the supplies and hand you the various grooming utensils. But because Poms need to be handled gently, the physical parts of grooming should be left to adults.

## Nail Care and Trimming

Nail care is often overlooked but an essential part of your Pomeranian's grooming routine. Overgrown toenails can cause limping and the feet to splay or can twist the joints of the toes causing toe arthritis. This is particularly a problem in older, less active Pomeranians because running on pavement often helps keep nails short. Since nails can grow at the rate of 2mm per week, nails that are not worn down can eventually penetrate the underside of the toe and become a problem.

*Towel dry him before you remove him from the bath.*

There are several types of nail clippers for you to choose from—"guillotine" type or scissors type. Find the smallest one for your Pom's tiny toes, and make sure it has a safety guard to prevent you from cutting the nails too short.

### How?

To get started, place your dog on your lap. Hold one of his paws in your hand and look at the nail. You should be able to see where the nail curves. Snip the nail off just before the curve. If you go any deeper, you will cut the "quick," the blood vessel inside the nail that bleeds when cut. On a white nail, the pink quick is easy to see, but on a black nail it's

not, so err on the side of caution. If you do accidentally cut the quick you can stop the bleeding with styptic powder.

It can sometimes be difficult to get your Pomeranian used to having his nails or feet touched. A good way to start is to touch one foot while he is sleeping. If he wakes up, remain casual about the touch and remove your hand. Anytime he resists, don't react negatively, just remove your grasp and try again at another time. Repeat this process often and over time your Pomeranian will be comfortable with the sensation. If you feel too nervous cutting his nails or he continues to resist having his feet touched, it would be a good idea to find a professional groomer.

### Dewclaws

Dewclaws are the "fifth finger" on your Pomeranian's front legs. Since he essentially walks on his toes, the dewclaw usually dangles several inches above the ground. The dewclaw can catch on brush, logs, rocks, or other obstructions the dog has to navigate over, under, or around. A torn dewclaw can bleed a lot, but generally it isn't a serious injury. If it does bleed, apply pressure and then wrap gauze around the dewclaw and leg.

*Find a small pair of nail clipper's for your Pomeranian's tiny feet.*

Pomeranians

Don't wrap too tightly, however, or you'll constrict blood flow into the lower leg.

## Paw Problems

The skin on your Pomeranian's feet is a common location for diseases. If his paws are not regularly exercised from puppyhood, growth abnormalities and claw problems can appear. Over-use (such as excessive walking on hard surfaces) can lead to tenderness and infection. There are dry skin treatments available to combat such problems.

You should check your Pomeranian's feet regularly to make sure that there are no splinters or infections in the paw area. An unusual smell or excretion coming from the paws may indicate infection. If he has a splinter, signs include limping or holding up a paw when sitting. If your Pomeranian appears to be in pain or you believe he might have an infection, the best thing to do is to take him to the veterinarian.

You should see your veterinarian if:

- More than one nail is cracked
- Your Pomeranian is having trouble walking, getting up, or climbing stairs
- One or more of his legs are dragging
- He has a limp
- There is swelling in the toes, feet, or legs
- Your Pomeranian is constantly

# SENIOR DOG TIP

## Grooming the Older Pomeranian

Proper grooming of older dogs is critical to ensure their heath and make them less susceptible to disease. Circulation and muscle tone decline in older dogs; therefore, you'll need to help out your older Pom with daily grooming sessions. This also allows the older dog to receive much needed physical contact and attention, which will allow him to maintain good health and spirits.

licking or biting his feet
- There are cuts, blisters, growths, or burns on his paw pads
- He has pain when jumping off a bed or changing position

Remember, the best preventative care is to trim his nails frequently.

## Ear Care

Your Pomeranian's ears should be cleaned once a month, more if he's prone to ear problems. Using a cotton ball soaked in mineral oil, clean the outer part of the ear only. Don't use a cotton swab, and never force anything

Looking Good

into the ear. Clean, odor-free, a pale pink color, and minimal accumulation of wax are indications of healthy ears.

## Eye Care

A healthy Pomeranian's eyes should be clear and bright—free of dirt, discharge, and inflammation. Clean the area around your Pomeranian's eyes daily with a cotton ball or clean cloth. Pomeranians tend to collect eye discharge, which can stain their coat so regular cleaning of the eye area is important. Any type of thick discharge is not normal and should be brought to your veterinarian's attention.

## Dental Care

Pomeranians are born with no teeth, but grow them in the first two or three weeks after birth. At around eight weeks of age, a puppy

should have a full set of twenty-eight teeth. At about three months of age, he will start to lose his first set of teeth. The adult tooth will start to appear within a few days of losing the "baby" tooth. When the process is complete, he will have a full set of forty-two teeth.

Gum disease is very common in dogs and especially common in toy dogs, who tend to have crowded mouths. Many dogs over the age of two or three have either gingivitis or periodontitis. Periodontitis, or periodontal disease, is the most common dental problem for dogs. It is caused by plaque, a mixture of bacteria, food debris, and cell mucus. It forms a milky-white film on the teeth and gums. If allowed to progress, the bacteria eventually eat away at the bone that holds the teeth in place. When mixed with saliva in the mouth, plaque turns into tartar.

The best way to prevent periodontal disease is to eliminate plaque before it becomes tartar. And the best way to do this is to brush your Pomeranian's teeth regularly. Brushing reduces the amount of bacteria in his mouth, which also has the benefit of making his breath smell fresher.

*Clean the area around your Pomeranian's eyes daily.*

## Brush Up!

Toothpaste formulated specifically for dogs is available at any pet store. Don't use human toothpaste—he cannot spit it out as a human would, and human toothpaste can cause an upset stomach. Beef and liver flavored toothpastes are available that many dogs find yummy.

There are also a number of dog toothbrush styles; just make sure to buy the smallest size. Pomeranians' teeth touch in one or two places only, and their teeth are narrow. A dog toothbrush reaches 90% of the area that needs to be cleaned, but doesn't always reach the teeth that are farthest back in your Pomeranian's mouth. This is okay—it's not the most important area, and chewing on a cotton rope bone can help clean those back teeth. Or, you can use finger brush instead of a toothbrush. A finger brush fits onto your fingertip and lets you brush your Pomeranian's teeth almost without him knowing it.

## How?

Begin the brushing process by finding a nice, quiet place where both you and your Pomeranian can be relaxed. Hold him as if you are cuddling him and gently stroke the outside of his cheeks with your finger. Once he becomes comfortable with the motion, place some toothpaste on your finger and let him taste it. Finally, place some toothpaste on the brush and begin cleaning only a few teeth at a time. Over the course of a week you can brush more and more teeth as he becomes more familiar with the process. Remember to go slowly and stop each session before he gets too uncomfortable. Praise him lavishly once you are done.

You should have his teeth professionally cleaned every so often

## The Expert Knows

### How to Select a Groomer

Some people prefer to leave grooming to the professionals. Here's how to find a groomer:

1. Get referrals from your veterinarian, friends, and family. Word of mouth is often the best way to locate an effective groomer.
2. Ask questions of your potential groomer, like did you attend a grooming school? Are you a member of a professional organization? How long have you been in business? Do you have photos of your work?
3. Tour the facility. Make sure it is clean and organized. Also note whether there are any foul odors. Is the staff friendly and knowledgeable?

Looking Good

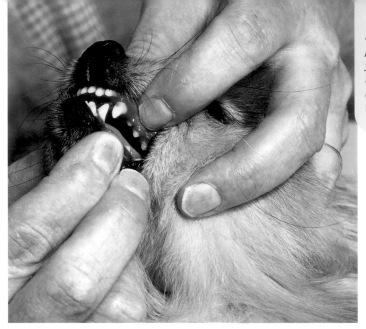

48

scrape the tarter off your Pomeranian's teeth. Just remember any time you give your dog a bone you must supervise him to prevent a choking accident.

There are also a multitude of dental toys available for your Pomeranian. Some types include dental chews, plaque attacker balls, and dental rings—all of which contain ground bone which helps remove plaque and tarter, strengthen enamel, prevent tooth decay, and whiten teeth.

The second biggest problem for dogs and their teeth is breakage which can cause infections within the tooth. Pomeranians can break their teeth easily, so be leery of feeding any tough or hard substances to your Pomeranian.

by your veterinarian. A veterinarian will anesthetize your Pomeranian, scrape all of the plaque buildup from above and below the gum line, and then polish the teeth.

## Other Dental Problems

Another dental problem to be aware of is gingivitis, or gum disease. Gingivitis is an inflammation of the gum tissue; it does not affect the deeper structures of the teeth. Without treatment, gingivitis can lead to periodontitis, bone loss, loosening of the teeth, and eventually loss of teeth. Bad breath often indicates gum disease. Feeding dry food and some dental bones can help maintain his dental hygiene. A good raw marrow bone or knuckle bone can help keep your Pomeranian's teeth free of tartar. The gnawing motion can effectively

## Attire and Accessories

Although clothes aren't a necessity, some owners of small breeds enjoy dressing up their dogs. There are countless dog apparel companies who can help you dress your Pomeranian for any and every occasion. You can choose between Halloween costumes, sweaters, coats, hair accessories, hats, and paw protectors—your Pomeranian is sure to be the most stylish dog on the block.

But these items are not only just fashion statements. Some have important functions as well. Paw protectors are a good choice in the winter months as most Pomeranians cannot tolerate wet, cold snow for long periods of time.

Any clothing you purchase for your Pomeranian should fit him properly—not too loose or too small. Clothing that is too big can make it difficult for him to move freely and can cause him to become entangled. Clothing that is too tight can restrict his movement and could even be painful. Never force your Pomeranian to wear something he's not comfortable in, and don't leave him dressed up while he is unattended. Make sure the clothing material is breathable and comfortable so your Pomeranian won't mind looking his best every day of the week.

*You can dress up your Pomeranian for any occasion.*

# Chapter 5

# Feeling Good

In general, Pomeranians are a healthy, long-lived breed. If you are careful about the veterinarian and visit him or her diligently, your Pomeranian will, indeed, be a long-time companion. Keep in mind that just like children, Pomeranians don't look forward to visiting their doctors. My own Pom, Pierre, is no exception, so it was important to find a friendly, gentle veterinarian. Pierre's veterinarian is always kind to him and speaks to him in a quiet voice, which reduces Pierre's stress and makes him feel more comfortable in the doctor's arms. Take your time and find a vet who meets both your and your dog's needs.

## Finding a Veterinarian

Your veterinarian should be chosen with as much care as your family doctor. It can be a long process, but it is a critical one. Most veterinarians belong to a local medical association—you can check your local association for current information on nearby veterinarians. All veterinarians are required to attend continuing education programs in order to maintain their licenses.

A good way to find a veterinarian is by word of mouth. Talk to friends, family, and coworkers with pets. If you purchased your Pom from a breeder, you can check with the breeder, who may be able to refer you to a veterinarian who specializes in Pomeranians.

Consider where the veterinarian is located when making your decision; you don't want to travel far if your dog is sick or injured. Another consideration is office hours. Find out what days they are open and if they have evening hours. Visit the office, too, to make sure it's clean and organized and the staff is friendly, helpful, and knowledgeable. Don't forget to ask about emergency care, as well as asking if the vet is familiar with Pomeranians. Ask also about vaccination protocols for puppies and adult dogs.

Once you've found the right vet, do set up a regular program of preventive care for your Pomeranian, so the

*Once you've found the right vet, set up a regular program of preventive care for your Pomeranian.*

veterinarian will be familiar with him and have current records. If possible, make sure every veterinarian in the practice has met your dog at least once so that both dog and doctor will know what to expect. If the practice you choose does not have 24-hour emergency care, ask for a recommendation of the closest hospital that does.

## Puppy's First Visit

A lot will happen at your Pomeranian's

Pomeranians

first visit to the vet's office. Filling out paperwork about both you and your dog will be the first order of business. Once they have all of your vital information, a technician will escort you into the exam room, weigh your Pom, take his temperature and listen to his heart. When the veterinarian comes in, he or she will ask you a series of questions, such as how long you have owned your Pomeranian, where you got him, what type of food he is eating, and how often? Then, he will begin the physical exam. Your veterinarian will look in his eyes and ears and examine his teeth. Next, he will check his skin for abnormalities, fleas and/or ticks. He will then feel his abdomen for enlarged organs and the belly button for a possible hernia. Next he will listen to your Pomeranian's heart and lungs. The joints on his knees will also be checked. Finally, he will check his genitals for any abnormalities. The veterinarian will also talk about a vaccination schedule.

After the physical exam is complete, your veterinarian will ask if you have any questions. This is a good time to bring up any concerns you may have about training, feeding, or playing with your new Pomeranian.

## The Annual Visit

During the annual visit, your veterinarian will check your Pomeranian's nose for any unusual discharge and his eyes to make sure they're free of debris, bright, and without infection. He or she will go on to check your dog's mouth for lumps, cuts, and the condition of his teeth. Ears will be checked to ensure they are mite-free. Your vet will also listen to your Pomeranian's chest and heart, and check his skin and coat for fleas or ticks. Finally, your Pomeranian's abdomen will be checked for any lumps or distention.

Following the physical exam, your veterinarian may order a lab evaluation which could include a urinalysis, complete blood cell count and/or a fecal exam.

## Vaccinations

Immunizing your Pomeranian against disease would seem to be a simple process—but don't take it for granted. It is important to stay current with your Pomeranian's vaccinations to keep him happy, healthy, and with you for many, many years.

Vaccinations work by stimulating your Pomeranian's immune system to produce specific antibodies to fight a subsequent attack by the disease. Vaccines come in two forms: modified live formulas that include a weakened form of the disease and killed or inactivated formulas that have an additional substance called an adjuvant added to boost the immune response. Each has its advantages. Modified live vaccines can cause swift development of long-lasting immunity but may

53

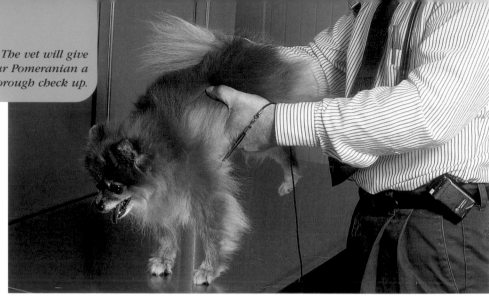

The vet will give your Pomeranian a thorough check up.

produce mild cases of illness. Killed vaccines are more stable, have a longer shelf life, and do not produce mild infections, but the protection may not last as long.

For young puppies, vaccinations usually start at six-to-eight weeks of age and are given every three-to-four weeks until the puppy is 16 weeks of age. A minimum of two multivalent vaccinations (including distemper and parvo) given three to four weeks apart are required for every puppy over three months old. In the US, an additional vaccination against rabies is also necessary. Rabies vaccination is required by law at local or state levels because the disease is fatal to humans as well as other mammals. Some veterinarians use three-year rabies vaccine; those in areas with disease outbreaks give boosters every year for maximum protection.

It is possible for your Pomeranian to have a systemic reaction to a vaccine, including a low-grade fever or muscle aches and pain. This reaction is more common in young dogs and causes them to eat less and sleep more for 24-48 hours.

Vaccination protocols have changed over the past few years. Worries about overvaccinating have led many vets to stop automatic yearly booster shots. Some holistic vets believe vaccinating too often can be counterproductive and cause adverse reactions and eventually compromise your Pomeranian's long-term health. It is important to ask your veterinarian questions to ensure your dog is receiving only those vaccines that are necessary. You can ask your veterinarian to check antibodies before the vaccination to confirm the shot is required.

## Diseases to Vaccinate Against

Rabies, distemper, parvovirus, hepatitis, parainfluenza, and coronavirus are major viral diseases affecting dogs. Lyme disease, leptospirosis, and a type of kennel cough (bordetella) are bacterial diseases. Each of these diseases can be prevented by judicious vaccination.

- **Rabies**: A deadly neurological virus transmitted through the bite of an infected animal. The rabies vaccine is mandatory in the US.

- **Distemper:** The American Veterinary Medical Association considers canine distemper to be the greatest single disease threat to the world's dog population. Highly contagious, it attacks the nervous system, often causing partial or complete paralysis as well as seizures. Most distemper cases occur in dogs less than six months and in old dogs that have not been routinely vaccinated. Once a dog is infected, there is no cure.

- **Parvovirus (Parvo):** a highly contagious virus that affects the intestine, bone marrow, and lymphoid tissue, this deadly disease is transmitted through the feces of infected dogs.

- **Hepatitis:** a serious disease caused by the adenovirus that affects the white blood cell count, and the kidneys and liver.

- **Coronavirus:** A virus related to the human cold, this contagious disease is most serious in puppies.

Symptoms including vomiting, diarrhea, and depression. This vaccine is usually only recommended in areas where the virus is prevalent.

- **Lyme disease:** caused by a bacteria carried by the deer tick, this disease causes lameness, fever, and heart and kidney disease. This vaccine is optional, recommended if you live in an endemic area and your dog spends a lot of time in the woods.

- **Leptospirosis (Lepto):** a bacterial infection that affects the liver and kidney. Not all veterinarians

**FAMILY-FRIENDLY TIP**

**Bring the Kids!**

Kids and puppies can be a great combination when the children are educated about puppy care. A great place to start is to bring your child with you to your dog's veterinary visits. Your child will learn things about your Pomeranian during the course of the exam and will also have an opportunity to ask their own questions of the doctor. It is important to remember that Pomeranians can be afraid of a child's yelling and squealing so ask your child to remain calm during his exam.

*Talk to your vet about your Pom's vaccination schedule.*

recommend this vaccination. Talk to your vet about your options.

- **Kennel cough:** the name for respiratory disease in dogs that covers the actions of several infectious agents, including Bordatella bronchiseptica, a bacteria, canine adenovirus-2, and canine parainfluenza virus. Kennel cough is highly contagious, especially in kennels or shelters where canine immune systems are stressed. Adequate ventilation helps keep the infections in check, but the only sure measure of prevention is vaccination.

## Pomeranian-Specific Illnesses

Most Pomeranians live out their lives in good health. However, every breed is prone to certain diseases, and the Pom is no exception.

## Black Skin Disease (Alopecia X)

Black skin disease, also known as "Alopecia X" is hair loss caused by a hormone imbalance. It occurs in many of the spitz breeds, like the Siberian Husky, Chow Chow, and Pomeranian. The long hair is lost first, then the undercoat. The bald skin then turns black, but it is not painful or itchy for the dog.

Your veterinarian will do some tests to rule out other disorders like Cushing's disease or hypothyroidism. If it is neither of these conditions, and your vet diagnoses your dog with black skin disease, there are treatments available. Since this condition seems to mostly affect unneutered animals, the first step is to have the Pomeranian spayed or neutered. Many dogs fully recover their hair after the operation.

If neutering does not work, there are medications available. Your vet can advise you. Keep in mind this is a cosmetic condition, and your dog is not being harmed.

## Collapsing Trachea

Breathing disorders (collapsing tracheas) are fairly common illnesses in Pomeranians. The trachea or windpipe is comprised of cartilage rings joined by muscles and ligaments. The cartilage rings make the trachea rigid so that air can freely pass to the lungs. Sometimes the rigid cartilage rings become soft or thin. When your Pomeranian inhales air, the rings collapse causing breathing difficulties. In severe cases, death may result. What are the symptoms of a collapsed trachea? Chronic sporadic coughing or coughing with a "goose honking"-type sound, and breathing difficulties.

Veterinarians don't definitively know exactly what causes collapsing trachea. Chronic bronchitis, obesity, and tracheal injury can contribute to the disease. Minor cases of collapsing trachea may respond to medication. Other cases may respond to surgery where a plastic device is implanted to prevent collapse.

Is there any way to prevent the trachea from collapsing? You can make sure your Pomeranian has the proper nutrition to keep his immune system strong and avoid stresses which lead to chronic bronchitis. Make sure your

## The Expert Knows

### Neutering Your Pomeranian

Most shelters and virtually all rescue groups sterilize dogs before making them available to adopters. Neutering has many benefits. Male dogs are usually better pets—they have less desire to roam, to mark territory (including furniture), or to exert dominance over family members. They are also healthier pets: no chance of developing testicular cancer, which is not uncommon among aging intact male dogs.

Females also tend to be better pets if they do not experience estrus every six-to-nine months. Heat cycles bring hormonal changes that can lead to personality changes. Repeated heat cycles subject the reproductive system to uterine and mammary cancers and uterine infections.

• Start a chew toy habit. If he gets in the practice of chewing on toys, it will keep his teeth much cleaner. Just make sure the toys do not have small pieces that could be chewed off and become a choking hazard.

• Feed him a premium dry food. Canned food, low-quality foods that contain sugar, and many commercially prepared "doggie treats" promote tooth decay.

• Give marrow bones often.

• If your Pomeranian's teeth have tartar buildup, the only way get them completely clean is to have them professionally cleaned at your veterinarian's office.

## Retained Deciduous Teeth

Retained deciduous teeth is the most common orthodontic problem in small dogs. It usually happens as a result of an adult tooth putting pressure on the base of the baby tooth, causing a problem within the root structure. When this happens, the adult tooth does not line up correctly with the deciduous tooth. Therefore, there is no pressure for the baby tooth to fall out. This forces the adult tooth to the side and now two teeth are present. Since the gum is not formed correctly, plaque can build up around the misaligned teeth. Finally, the adult tooth can become impacted. This condition can be treated by the extraction of the deciduous tooth. The extraction should be done as soon as the adult tooth is seen erupting.

Pomeranian maintains proper body weight and avoid pulling too hard on his leash, which can contribute to tracheal injury.

## Dental Problems

Pomeranians are prone to early tooth loss. The most commonly occurring problems for this breed involve the teeth (including periodontitis and gingivitis) which, if not scrupulously cared for and maintained through frequent cleaning, can fall out at a relatively early age.

The following are some suggestions for avoiding early tooth loss:

## Ear Problems

While Pomeranians don't have the same amount of ear problems as floppy-eared dogs, like Basset Hounds, ear problems can still plague this tiny breed. The signs of ear problems are:

- Unpleasant odor
- Excessive scratching and/or pawing of the ear
- Sensitivity to touch
- Constant tilting/shaking of the head
- Black or yellowish discharge
- Redness or swelling of the ear flap or canal
- Changes in behavior like listlessness, depression, or irritability
- Accumulation of dark brown wax
- Loss of balance or hearing

### Ear Infections

Otitis externa, an infection of the external ear canal, and otitis media, an infection of the middle ear, are usually caused by bacteria or yeast. If your Pomeranian has an ear infection, he will be in considerable pain and discomfort. Your veterinarian will prescribe antibiotics for the bacterial infections and antifungals for yeast infections. Ear infections can also be indicative of other problems such as allergies, hormonal abnormalities, or hereditary diseases. Your veterinarian will determine the cause during your visit and will recommend the appropriate follow-up care.

### Ear Mites

Your Pomeranian may have ear mites, which are highly contagious common parasites, often contracted from pet to pet. Excessive itching is the most common sign. Ear mites create dark, crumbly debris that look like coffee grinds in the ears. If your veterinarian finds ear mites he will clean out the wax in your Pomeranian's ear and massage in an antibiotic into it. A follow-up treatment by the veterinarian

*A good dental chew helps keep your dog's teeth and gums healthy.*

within four weeks will be necessary to get any remaining mites or mite eggs out of the ear. It can sometimes be necessary for you to administer antibiotics in his ear at home for period of time.

The best prevention against mites or infections is regular ear cleaning (see Chapter 4 for more information on cleaning your Pom's ears).

### Administering Ear Drops

Should your Pomeranian need ear drops, here are some tips for administering the medicine:

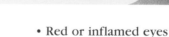

*Keep a look out for any changes in your Pom's ears—redness or a strong smell indicate a problem.*

1. Clean the external ear thoroughly with a moistened cotton ball using a veterinarian-recommended solution. Read the label instructions carefully for correct dosage.
2. Gently hold the ear, squeeze out the desired amount, and apply it to the lowest part of the ear canal.
3. Gently massage the ear area to help work the medication deeper into the ear canal. If there is enough medication in the ear, you will just begin to hear a "squishing" noise as you massage.

### Eye Problems

This breed can experience certain eye problems. Common symptoms of eye illness are:

- Red or inflamed eyes
- Matter "stuck" on the surface or in the corners of the eye
- Cloudy or dull eye surface
- The third eyelid visibly coming across the eye

### Conjunctivitis

Conjunctivitis is an inflammation of the membrane that covers both the inner lining of the eyelid and the white of the eye. It may be caused by infections, allergies, inadequate tear production, or irritation. Your veterinarian will treat conjunctivitis with topical antibacterial medications. If other symptoms are present in your Pomeranian, oral antibiotics may be administered.

Keratoconjunctivitis Sicca—or dry eye—occurs when the tear glands cannot provide your Pomeranian's eyes with enough tears. Viral diseases, drug reactions, allergies, or injuries may lead to this condition which, if chronic, can cause loss of vision. If your Pomeranian is suffering from dry eye, your veterinarian will start treatment with artificial tears and lubricants. Topical antibiotics may be necessary if the lubricant does not clear up the problem. Treatment for dry eye is typically a long-term process.

### Corneal Ulceration

Corneal ulceration can result when the cornea's surface is scratched by a foreign object or is damaged by inadequate tear production or bacterial infection. Aging dogs can be prone to this problem. Pomeranians who have corneal ulceration will be treated by their veterinarians with topical antibiotics and possibly pupil dilators. Ulcers should heal within three to five days.

### Cataracts and Glaucoma

Pomeranians, just like humans, can have these serious eye diseases. Cataracts cloud the lens inside the eye and are the most common cause of canine blindness. Glaucoma stems from too much pressure being exerted upon the eye's interior as a result of a decrease in the amount of fluid draining from it. If your Pomeranian

suffers from glaucoma, treatment will usually involve attempts to decrease the production of fluid within the eye. Both topical and systemic medications will be administered by your veterinarian. Surgery is also available if a tumor is the cause of the glaucoma. Cataracts are removed by a machine which uses ultrasonic sound waves to break down and remove the lens from your Pomeranian's eye. New, synthetic lenses are then implanted.

### Entropion

Another potential eye problem your Pomeranian may experience is entropion—an abnormal in-rolling of the eyelid. Usually an inherited problem, it forms in young adult Pomeranians. Most dogs with entropion

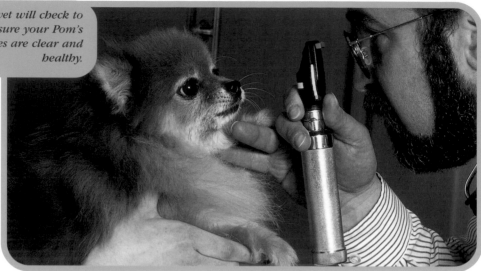

*Your vet will check to make sure your Pom's eyes are clear and healthy.*

require surgery, which involves removing a small portion of the skin to tighten the eyelid.

### Progressive Retinal Atrophy

Retinal atrophy is another possible eye disorder your Pomeranian could be susceptible to. This inherited eye disease is characterized by abnormal development or premature deterioration of your Pomeranian's retina. Unfortunately, there is no therapy available at this time to prevent, slow the progression of, or reverse the changes caused by retinal atrophy. If your Pomeranian is faced with this disease, the best course of action is to make him comfortable by placing night-lights throughout the home, avoiding moving furniture so he can memorize the layout of the house, place barriers in front of stairs so he

won't fall, and buy toys that make noise to encourage him to play.

### Administering Eye Drops

If your Pomeranian needs eye drops, here are some tips to administer them:

- Remove any discharge around the eye with a cotton ball moistened with saline solution.
- See the instructions on the bottle for dosage. Shake if necessary.
- Use one hand to hold the bottle between thumb and index and place the other under your Pomeranian's jaw to support the head.
- Tilt his head back, and to prevent blinking, use your free fingers to hold the eyelids open.
- Hold the bottle close to the eye but DON'T touch the eye's surface.

- Squeeze the drops on to the eyeball and then release the head.
- Your Pomeranian will blink, spreading the medication over the eye's surface.

## Hypoglycemia

Another disease which may affect your Pomeranian is hypoglycemia, also referred to as low blood sugar. Pomeranians have a very small fat reserve, which in times of excitement and stress is used up very rapidly. Signs of hypoglycemia include confusion, disorientation, unusual drowsiness, shivers, and/or staggering. In an advanced stage your Pomeranian can collapse and go into seizures. If this happens, immediate sugar and protein ingestion is necessary, as is a trip to the vet. In an emergency, sugar or honey will work.

If your Pomeranian experiences such an episode, contact your veterinarian.

## Luxating Patella

Another condition which may affect your Pomeranian is luxating patellas or dislocating kneecaps. This is a disorder of the kneecap in which the knee will slip out of place when the dog moves. There are varying degrees of this disorder, with the most severe requiring surgery. This condition can either be congenital (present at birth) or acquired (trauma induced). Pomeranians who experience patellar luxation will most likely develop arthritis in the future.

## General Illnesses

Unfortunately, Pomeranians do get sick. Your Pomeranian may get sick from parasites, viruses, bacteria, protozoa, and fungus or food poisoning. In some cases, these diseases and infestations are fatal unless caught early and treated. Fortunately, veterinarian researchers have developed drugs and treatments that reduce the occurrence and effects of many diseases and parasites, but they have not eradicated them.

How do you know if your Pomeranian is sick? The American Veterinary Medical

*Clean grass and pollen from your Pom's eyes after he's been outside.*

Feeling Good

Association says to call your veterinarian if your Pomeranian shows any of the following signs:

- Abnormal discharges from the nose, eyes, or other body openings.
- Abnormal behavior, sudden viciousness, or lethargy.
- Abnormal lumps, limping, or difficulty getting up or lying down.
- Loss of appetite, marked weight losses or gains, or excessive water consumption.
- Difficult, abnormal, or uncontrolled waste elimination.
- Excessive head shaking, scratching, and licking or biting any part of the body.
- Dandruff, loss of hair, open sores, or a ragged or dull coat.
- Foul breath or excessive tarter deposits on teeth.

## First Aid Supplies

- Gauze sponges
- Antibiotic ointment
- Rubbing alcohol
- Ear syringe
- Ace self-adhering athletic bandage
- Petroleum jelly
- Eye wash
- Sterile, non-adherent pads
- Anti-diarrhea tablets
- Antihistamine capsules
- Hydrocortisone acetate
- Sterile stretch gauze bandage
- Hydrogen peroxide
- Bandage scissors

## Cancer

As our Pomeranians are living longer, veterinarians are seeing more cases in cancer in their senior patients. Some types are more curable and treatable than others. The type of treatment for cancer depends on the type of cancer your Pomeranian has developed, the stage of the cancer, and its location. If cancer is suspected, your veterinarian will do a biopsy. If it proves cancerous, chemotherapy or surgery will be used. Pills, injections, and IVs can all be used to treat your Pomeranian. Dogs who receive chemotherapy should be able

to perform and enjoy all their normal activities.

The American Veterinary Medical Association lists these ten common signs of cancer in small animals:

1. Abnormal swelling that persists or continues to grow
2. Sores that do not heal
3. Weight loss
4. Loss of appetite
5. Bleeding or discharge from any body opening
6. Offensive odor
7. Difficulty eating or swallowing

8. Hesitation to exercise or loss of stamina
9. Persistent lameness or stiffness
10. Difficulty breathing, urinating, or defecating

## Parasites

### *Fleas*

Fleas are a common annoyance for dog owners. Dr. Galob points out, "Normally only adult fleas live on pets, and often they remain there only long enough to feed. Eggs may be laid on the pet, but usually fall off the pet into the environment where conditions are right for them to develop (through a multistage life cycle) into adult fleas. As a result, it is possible to have a substantial flea problem although you have only identified a few or no fleas on your pet. Egg and larval stages can survive in your home all year and in your yard from spring through late fall (all year in warmer climates). Biting and scratching on the lower back, tail, and abdomen are the most common signs of flea infestation, and dermatitis will often flare up in these areas. Flea control involves treatment of the pet and the environment by means of shampoos, sprays, dips, powders, oral medications, and collars. Your veterinarian can recommend the most appropriate flea prevention/treatment program for your pet. Fleas carry tapeworms, so be sure to have your veterinarian check your pet for these intestinal parasites as well."

## Beware of Pesticides

Misuse or overuse of pesticides and harsh chemicals can be harmful to your Pomeranian. Try the following tips to limit his exposure:

1. Before you use a product, read the label carefully to be sure it is pet friendly.
2. Always use the recommended amount, never more.
3. Check for side effects in your Pomeranian after using any new product.
4. Shop around—there are manyorganic products available that are safe to use around your Pomeranian.

### *Ticks*

Ticks are also a potential problem for your Pomeranian. "Ticks are not only an irritant and nuisance to your pet but may transmit several debilitating diseases, such as Lyme disease, babesiosis, and ehrlichiosis. Many flea prevention/treatment products will also help with control of ticks," says Dr. Galob. "Owners whose dogs have substantial exposure to ticks (e.g., sporting dogs, dogs that go camping, and those spending time in forest preserves or woods) should also ask their veterinarian's advice about the appropriateness of a vaccination for Lyme disease.

65

66

The best way to remove a tick that has found its way onto your Pomeranian is to a get a pair of tweezers, pull the surrounding hairs away, and grasp the tick as close to its head as possible. Do not squeeze the tick—pull up and away from your Pomeranian gently, trying not to break the head of the tick off. Once removed, flush the tick down the toilet. Be sure to wash your hands and your Pomeranian's skin thoroughly with anti-bacterial soap. If you suspect some tick remains in him, see your veterinarian immediately.

## Worms

- **Heartworms:** parasites transmitted by mosquitoes that can potentially be fatal to your Pomeranian. Gail Galob, DVM, warns, "Have your dog or cat tested for the presence of heartworms by your veterinarian and ask about heartworm preventatives. Treatment for this disease can be expensive and risky for your pet. Prevention is easy and inexpensive. The fact that your dog only goes outside to urinate and defecate, or the fact that your cat does not go outside at all, does not eliminate the risk of disease. Mosquitoes are everywhere!"

- **Hookworms:** these worms attach to the intestinal wall of your dog and cause bleeding and anemia. Hookworms can be transmitted to humans through the skin. Some puppies are born with hookworms in their system.

- **Roundworms:** the most common worm found in dogs. Almost all puppies are born with roundworms. These spaghetti-like worms are carried through the bloodstream to the liver, lungs, and trachea.

- **Whipworms:** this worm causes intermittent diarrhea in your dog. This worm is very hard to get rid of. Found in the soil, it can withstand very cold weather and can lay dormant for a very long time.

## Alternative Therapies

Nonconventional therapy for dogs is becoming more and more mainstream as a greater number of veterinarians are embracing new holistic treatments into their practice. Holistic medicine combines conventional veterinary medicine with additional therapies to address an illness. These holistic treatments can provide a more natural way for your dog's body to heal. Some treatments include acupuncture, homeopathy, massage, and herbology. Those veterinarians who practice nonconventional treatments often do so to allow them to take a "whole picture" of the dog— the environment, the disease, the relationship between you and your Pomeranian. Alternative veterinarians attempt to discover the

underlying cause of illness and then treat it with a non-invasive, drugless approach.

## Acupuncture

Acupuncture, a traditional Chinese therapeutic technique whereby the body is punctured with fine needles to achieve a desired healing effect, has been used to treat both humans and animals for thousands of years. Acupuncture is used to help stimulate nerves and increase blood circulation which, in turn, can help the body heal itself. Veterinarians who use acupuncture often do so as a form of pain modification for the animal. If you chose to use this form of

*Check your dog for fleas and ticks after he's been outside.*

alternative therapy, The American Academy of Veterinary Acupuncture notes two very important criteria when choosing the best acupuncturist for your Pomeranian: "Your veterinarian acupuncturist must be a licensed veterinarian. In most states, provinces, and countries, veterinarian acupuncture is considered a surgical procedure that, legally, may only be administered by licensed veterinarians. Secondly, your veterinarian acupuncturist should have considerable formal training in the practice of animal acupuncture."

Check out www.aava.org to find a licensed veterinary acupuncturist near you.

### Herbs

Herbs can be used to help your Pomeranian heal—various problems like poor appetite, arthritis, parasites, and yeast infections all have herbal remedies. Some herbs are reputed to repel fleas, sooth irritated skin, and improve digestion. It is important to remember that your Pomeranian is small and has a short digestive system; therefore, digestion of an herb will work better and more swiftly than with a human or larger dog. Always check with your veterinarian first before you give your Pomeranian any herb. Not all herbs will agree with your Pomeranian so it is important to introduce no more than one herb a week.

## SENIOR DOG TIP

### Caring for Your Senior Pomeranian

You'll want to continue with your annual veterinary visits for your senior dog, and at some point your veterinarian may recommend scheduling appointments every six months to help catch any age-related problems early. Your vet will run blood tests to check the liver, kidneys, and pancreas, check your Pom's vision and hearing, and may suggest a special test to check the heart.

Arthritis may begin to creep up on your friend, so try to make him as comfortable as possible. He may need some extra help walking up stairs or getting out of the car. But remember he still needs exercise—it will keep his spirits up and can even help loosen tight muscles. Your veterinarian may recommend aspirin or other anti-inflammatory drugs to ease pain and stiffness. Keep his nails trimmed short and lay down rugs or non-skid mats on uncarpeted floors to reduce the risk of falls.

Some popular herbs and the ailments they treat include:

- peppermint for allergies
- lemonbalm for cancer
- echinacea for infectious diseases
- tea tree oil for skin problems
- goldenseal and olive oil for parasite control
- celery seed for bones and joints
- chamomile for nausea
- arrowroot for soothing bowels
- horsetail for urinary problems
- almond oil for ear troubles

## Homeopathy

Homeopathy is a natural alternative for healing that works by eliminating the underlying imbalance in the body that is causing the illness. Based on the idea that "like cures like," homeopathic remedies consist of micro doses of substances from plant, mineral, and animal sources that, in large doses, create the symptoms of the disease being treated. The homeopathic dose in the remedies, however, is so small that in some cases no molecule of the original substance remains. Individual remedies prescribed by a veterinarian may be dosed differently, and instructions should be followed carefully.

To find a holistic veterinarian that practices homeopathy near you, check the American Holistic Veterinary Medical Association (www.ahvma.org) or Academy of Veterinary Homeopathy (www.theavh.org) referral directories.

*You might want to explore some alterative therapies with your Pomeranian.*

# Chapter 6

# Being Good

You might be surprised at what your tiny dog is capable of. Many Pomeranians have competed successfully in obedience trials; trained as hearing assistance dogs; trained in search and rescue for use on sites where a small-sized dog is necessary (e.g., earthquake sites). Pomeranians have also been used very successfully as therapy dogs as well as consoling the sick and elderly in hospitals and nursing homes (you'll learn more about these activities in Chapter 8). But before these Poms were able to do any of these extraordinary accomplishments, they had to learn basic training. While the advanced training these skills need may not be up your alley, your Pomeranian needs to learn basic training as well. A well-behaved, well-socialized dog is a pleasure to be around and will make your Pom a true part of the family.

## Socialization

Pomeranians are very social dogs—in fact, their friendliness is one of their most endearing qualities. However, proper socialization is still important, even for the friendliest of breeds. Socialization is the process of exposing your Pomeranian to different types of people, sights, and sounds. Puppyhood, especially between the ages of 16 to 18 weeks, is the time of socialization. Take advantage of it by making sure your Pom has lots of positive experiences with the world. By beginning the socialization process early, you can train your Pomeranian to handle himself in busy/distracting situations. A well-socialized Pomeranian is not fearful of crowds and plays well with other dogs.

To socialize your Pomeranian, take him out as much as possible (wait until he is fully vaccinated before introducing him to other dogs). Get him used to children, the elderly, people with disabilities, and males and females of all races. Let him experience without fear trips to other people's homes, parks, stairs, noisy places—all on a leash, of course. Make sure the experiences are positive and happy.

## Other Dogs

Despite their small stature, Pomeranians are generally not frightened of much larger dogs. They don't seem to understand their own size and, thus, don't hesitate in defending themselves against a much larger dog. While it can sometimes be entertaining to watch your Pomeranian barking and acting brave around a much larger animal, make sure you have a firm grip on him or his leash. My own Pierre has come in contact with much larger dogs under many

*Socialize your Pom with other dogs.*

different circumstances. Some have been fun, friendly frolicking while other encounters have been much fiercer. It can be quite scary seeing your precious, tiny Pomeranian in a brawl with a much larger dog. It's important to keep an eye on your Pomeranian and make sure his collar is always on securely and his leash properly fastened so he will not escape your grip and leap into a potentially dangerous situation.

## Puppy Kindergarten

Puppy kindergarten is a great way for Pomeranian owners to train and socialize their new family member. The age range for the class is usually 8 to 18 weeks. Puppy kindergarten covers all the basic obedience commands (such as Sit, Stay, Down, Heel, Drop, Off, and Come) as well as puppy ownership basics, including socialization, handling, and problem-solving for chewing, play biting, barking, digging, stealing, pulling on the lead, and jumping. Most places ask for written confirmation of vaccinations, and staff will usually check to ensure your Pomeranian puppy is free of fleas before joining the class. You will likely be asked to bring a leash, collar, and treats to the class. All family members are usually encouraged to join your

## The Expert Knows

### How Long Can He Stay in the Crate?

Crates are not a prison, and your Pomeranian should not be locked away in it for hours at a time. It's not fair to ask any dog to hold it that long, especially one with a tiny bladder. Crate duration guidelines: 9-10 week old puppy: 30-60 minutes; 11-16 weeks old: 1-2 hours; 17 plus weeks: not more than 4 hours (maximum of 6 at night-time).

Pomeranian's kindergarten class. Your family and puppy will benefit if all receive the same information and training instructions. When choosing a class it is always good to consult with your veterinarian, friends, and family to get referrals.

## Crate Training

You might look at a crate and think "puppy prison"—but this just isn't true! When used responsibly, the crate can be a great training tool and your Pomeranian's special place to get away from it all. Dogs are den animals, and the crate can replicate the feeling of comfort and security

The Association of Pet Dog Trainers (APDT) has the following suggestions for finding a trainer:

**1** Training your dog should be fun! A competent instructor will allow and encourage you to observe a class prior to making the decision to enroll.

**2** A skilled class instructor will provide a clear explanation of each lesson; demonstrate the behavior(s) that students will be teaching to their dogs; provide clear instructions and written handouts on how to teach the behavior(s); give students ample time in class to begin practicing the day's lesson; and assist students individually with proper implementation of techniques.

**3** A skilled and professional trainer will encourage dialogue and be courteous to both canine and human clients alike.

**4** You want to be comfortable with the training tools and methods used by the instructor. A skilled and professional dog trainer employs humane training methods which are not harmful to the dog and/or handler, and avoids the practices of hanging, beating, kicking, shocking, and all similar procedures or training devices that could cause the dog great pain, distress, or that have imminent potential for physical harm.

**5** A good instructor will take care to protect your dog's health in a group setting. Ask if dogs and puppies are required to be vaccinated prior to class and, if so, which vaccines are required. Make sure you and your veterinarian are comfortable with the vaccination requirements.

**6** Current clients are a valuable source of information for you. Attending a group class gives you the opportunity to ask clients how they feel about their experience—if they are enjoying the class and feel that their training needs and goals are being met.

(Courtesy of the Association of Pet Dog Trainers, www.apdt.com)

that a den provides.

How can you get your dog used to the crate? Start him on a routine early (at about eight weeks). It is best to introduce your Pomeranian to the concept of the crate slowly. Leave the crate door open and let him explore it. You can help him along by throwing a few tasty treats inside. Don't shut the door when he's inside—allow him to come and go as he pleases. You can also start feeding your Pom meals in his crate, so he'll have a good association with it. After he seems comfortable, you can start closing the crate door for a few minutes. Then gradually extend the time by keeping him in there for two hour intervals. You can include special toys and treats to help make his "room" a pleasant place to stay. Give him a small treat every time he has to go into his crate.

Most Pomeranians will bark and complain during the first few days. Once they begin to accept this new restriction on their freedom, they will quiet down and eventually learn to enjoy it.

## Housetraining

The first few weeks of owning your Pomeranian puppy are probably the most challenging, yet the most important. Spending the extra time and effort to housetrain your puppy (or re-train your adopted dog) now will be rewarding in the future.

## Schedule

First and foremost when housetraining, you will need to establish a regular schedule for feeding your pup and taking him outside. What is a typical schedule for your Pom?

1. Take him out first thing in the morning.
2. Take him out a half hour after he's been fed.
3. Take him out after he's been playing or gotten excited.
4. Take him out after he wakes up from a nap.
5. Take him out before he goes to sleep at night.

Always take him out at these times. You'll also want to take him out any time you notice him circling or sniffing the floor—good indicators that he needs to go. In order to notice these "signs," it's important to confine your puppy when housetraining—don't let him wander around the house, where you can't keep an eye on him. You'll be likely to miss these signs of him needing to go, and an accident is bound to happen. Use baby gates to confine him to a room and his crate to keep him safe when he's napping.

When you are outside in the right place for him to relieve himself, use a cue phrase such as, "Go pee!" When your Pomeranian relieves himself outside, praise him enthusiastically. You may want to give him a treat. If he likes to play outside, allow a little playtime after he goes.

## Preventing Accidents

Here are some tips to help prevent accidents:

- Keep your Pomeranian in a safe place when you are not home or are asleep. A crate or small room with a baby-gate will work.

- Keep your Pomeranian in the same room with you. If you see him start to have an accident, say, "No, outside!" while you pick him up and run outside.

- If you find an accident in the house don't punish him for it. It is your responsibility to pick up on his cues that he has to go out.

- If he does soil inside, treat the spot deeply and thoroughly with a bacterial enzyme odor eliminator. If you can't get rid of the scent, it will draw him back to the spot and he will pee there again.

- Make sure your Pomeranian is eating top-quality dog food and is free of intestinal parasites such as roundworms, hookworms, coccidia, giardia. Any of these things can sabotage housetraining efforts. If he seems to be urinating abnormally take him to your veterinarian.

- Schedule his food and water at appropriate times. Give water whenever you can, but not in the crate and not right before bed.

Almost every Pomeranian can be housetrained, if you do it right. However, some take longer than others. If you are minimizing the accidents by providing the proper supervision, and if you are treating any accident spots correctly, you should have success.

## Training

The best way to train your Pomeranian is with positive reinforcement. This means that you reward your dog when he does something or behaves in a way that you want. The reward can be a treat, praise, or even play—anything your Pomeranian really likes. Food is probably the most common reward used.

Why is positive training the best method for your dog? Pomeranians are spirited and spunky dogs, but they do have an innate desire to please you. Positive training takes this natural desire and turns it into a training tool—by rewarding him when he does

## SENIOR DOG TIP

### Training the Older Pomeranian

Training an older dog can be easier than training a puppy because they are calmer and can focus better. However, an older dog will already have some ingrained behaviors that may be hard to "unlearn." Housetraining older Pomeranians may take longer than younger ones, but it is not an impossible task. Just like puppies, older Pomeranians require gentle handling and positive reinforcement to train successfully.

something right, he gets the message that you are pleased with him, and nothing could make him happier!

Using punishment or fear to train your dog will just make him a scared and miserable dog—not only will you miss out on the great bond positive training fosters, punishment can often aggravate existing behavior problems. Never physically punish your dog! It's just not necessary. A firm "No!" when he's doing something you don't approve of is the best way to correct him.

## Treats for Training

Using food as a reward can be a powerful tool, but it can also cause problems. If the treats are too rich, your Pomeranian can develop an upset stomach. Feed him too many, and you could be on your way to an obese dog.

There are quite a few types of treats to choose from. Rolls, kibble, and freeze-dried treats are all good possibilities, as are tiny pieces of dog biscuit or Cheerios. Remember to keep the treat small so your Pomeranian can eat it quickly.

When training your Pomeranian, you want to move away from giving a food reward every time he completes something successfully. Start gradually replacing the treat with praise. Once he has learned a command, give the treat every other time, then every third time. Make sure your praise is lavish every time, with or without a treat. Pretty soon, your Pomeranian will work for praise—and the occasional snack.

## Basic Commands

Pomeranians should begin learning basic commands around three to four months old. You should do a little bit of training every day, for about 10 to 15 minutes. Keep the sessions short and fun, and end them before your Pomeranian gets bored or distracted.

Start training indoors, and then move outdoors when your Pomeranian is more reliable and less likely to be distracted. You'll need his regular leash, a longer leash (for teaching come), and a bag of treats. Timing is everything with training, so it's very important to reward your dog with a treat immediately after the desired behavior is performed.

### Sit

Teaching sit is a great first command, since it is one of the easiest. To teach the sit command, hold a small piece of treat at the level of his nose. He will smell the treat and move his head toward it. When he sniffs the food, slowly move your hand holding the food back and slightly over the top of his head, and say, "Sit." As soon as your Pomeranian sits, give him the treat while saying "Yes!", act very excited, and lavish him with praise.

### Come

You can start teaching your dog the come command even when you are sitting around the house. Any time you see your Pomeranian approaching you, use his name along with the command ("Pierre, Come"). When he reaches you, praise and pet him.

You can eventually start practicing this outside. With your dog on a long lead and in the sitting position, take a few quick steps back, and happily call out, "Pierre, Come." Praise and reward when he comes to

you. Gradually increase the distance between you.

Use a mild tone of voice when doing so your Pomeranian knows "come" is a positive action. And don't call your dog using the "Come" command for anything he might not like, such as nail clipping or going to the vet. Go get him when you need him for those things. He must only associate "come" with positive rewards. The come command can save his life—if he ever escapes and is running down the street, when you say "come" you need him to turn around and come back to you.

### Down

Down can be a little more difficult to teach than other commands, so have patience. Begin with your Pomeranian sitting in front of you. Hold a treat near his face, and then move the treat down to the floor. Wait a moment, holding the treat close to his body, and then move the treat slowly away, and say, "Down.". It may take several attempts for him to lie down. Once he does lie down, praise him, and give him his treat.

## Stay

Starting from the down position, hold out your hand with the palm up, say, "Stay," and take one step back. Avoid using food as a reward when teaching this command, as he will probably become too excited and unable to remain still. Release from the stay position a few seconds later and praise your Pomeranian.

## Heel

Begin with your Pomeranian sitting at your left side. With the leash gathered

## 10 Training Tips

1. Start training your Pomeranian puppy early. While older Pomeranians can be taught new tricks, what's learned earliest is often learned quickest and easiest.

2. Train your Pomeranian gently, and teach him using positive, motivational methods. Keep obedience sessions upbeat and fun.

3. Reinforce the desired behavior either through positive speech or by giving him a treat.

4. Always use your Pomeranian's name when speaking to him.

5. Avoid giving your Pomeranian commands that you know you cannot enforce. Every time you give a command that is neither complied with nor enforced he will come to learn that commands are optional.

6. One command should equal one response, so give your Pomeranian only one command then gently enforce it.

7. Avoid giving him combined commands which are incompatible such as "sit-down." This can confuse your Pomeranian. Say either "sit" or "down."

8. Use a soft voice when giving a command.

9. Whenever possible, use your Pomeranian's name positively, rather than using it in conjunction with reprimands or punishment.

10. Don't give your Pomeranian too much attention when he has misbehaved. If he receives a lot of attention when he jumps up on you, you are reinforcing the bad behavior.

(be sure it has slack in it) in your right hand, hold a treat directly in front of his nose with your left hand. Step out on your left foot as you walk briskly forward with your Pomeranian at a trot. Reward with the treat after only one or two steps.

## Leash Training

One of the most rewarding activities you can do with your Pomeranian is to go for leisurely walks. Before expecting him to calmly walk beside you on leash, you must first start by training him to be still when you are putting his collar and leash on.

Ask him to sit while you're putting on his leash. Most Pomeranians figure out that the leash means "fun outside time," and tremble with excitement, bark and run in circles after their leash is attached. If he immediately lunges toward the door simply hold onto the leash, stand still and let him spin in circles until he realizes that you're not going anywhere. He should then begin to calm down. When this happens, praise him. After another minute or so, begin walking your Pomeranian around your house to give him a chance to practice his "no-pulling" skills. Every time he pulls, lunges, or strains on the leash, simply stand still again. When he calms down, praise him (you can even feed him a treat). Try to keep his attention on you instead of the door that leads to outside.

When you feel that he is in control and is walking nicely without pulling in your house, then it is time to proceed outdoors. Walking outdoors provides much more distraction and excitement for your Pom, so you need to remain patient. Continue the process of remaining still when he lunges. He will learn quickly that walking nicely with no pulling gets him where he wants to go, and these outings can be some of his most exciting moments of the day.

## Tricks

These tricks are meant to be fun for you and your Pomeranian—none of them require special equipment. There are many ways to teach the same trick, so use the one that works best for you and your Pomeranian.

## Speak

This trick is usually a simple one to teach if your Pomeranian likes to bark (and what Pomeranian doesn't?). The trick is to get him to do it on command and from distances. First decide on a hand signal that is not similar to any other. Tell your Pomeranian to "speak" at the same time you use the signal. When he does bark, reward him with a treat immediately. If he doesn't bark readily, continue to give the command until he seems to get fed up with you and barks. Then quickly reward him.

## Wave

Begin with your Pomeranian in a sitting position. Decide on a hand signal. Sitting close to your Pomeranian give the command and hand signal, while nudging his paw until he lifts it up. Praise and reward him.

## Hide Your Eyes

Your Pomeranian can be in a sit or down position. The idea is to get him to cover his eyes with one paw on command. It will take some practice to find out the best method for your Pomeranian as all dogs respond differently to different signals. With treat in hand, tell him to "cover your eyes." Physically lift his paw over his muzzle and reward him. Another idea is to blow gently on his nose which will cause him to swipe at his face. When he does this, reward him.

## FAMILY-FRIENDLY TIP

### How to Involve your Child in Training

Here are some great tricks your child can teach your Pomeranian:

Shake Hands: Start by having your Pomeranian sit. Say, "Shake hands," and take his paw with your hand. Hold his paw and say, "Good dog!" Let go of his paw. Do this a few times every day.

Kiss: Every time your Pomeranian licks your face, say, "Give me a kiss. Good boy!" If he isn't a licker, put a little peanut butter on your cheek and say, "Give me a kiss." When he licks it off say, "Give me a kiss," again. Pomeranians generally are lickers so you might not even need the peanut butter—although that can be fun!

Fetch: If your Pomeranian doesn't fetch naturally, have an adult cut a slit in a tennis ball (or a smaller, rubber ball if that is too big). Put some treats inside the tennis ball. Show him that there are treats in there, and give him one. Then, throw the ball. In the beginning, run with him and get the ball; then give him the treat. Soon you will be able to throw the ball, and he will go get it.

81

Being Good

# Chapter 7

# In the

# Doghouse

Behind those loving eyes and cute expression can be a cunning, determined-not-to listen, out-right outlaw lurking. No matter how adorable your Pomeranian, there's a chance he could develop some type of problem behavior. Even my own wonderful Pierre has gone through the occasional housesoiling and ten minute barking fits (both very typical Pom problems). Whatever the problem behavior is, it is important to address it quickly so he doesn't become accustomed to the unwanted behavior.

*Time, perseverance, and training can help alleviate problem behaviors.*

Keep in mind your Pomeranian is not acting out of spite or to "get back" at you. Most problem behaviors are rooted in what is very normal dog behavior— barking, chewing, even nipping are all ways dogs express themselves. The "problem" comes when the behavior does not fit in with how we want our dogs to behave. If you are a good leader, consistent in your training, and attentive to your dog, you usually can avoid most problems with your Pomeranian.

## Dealing With Problems

If you notice a problem behavior, first take your Pomeranian to see a veterinarian. He may actually have an illness that is causing the unusual behavior (e.g., soiling in the house may be the result of a bladder infection).

Here are some steps to take when dealing with problems:

- Note the location of the problem behavior—was it in the car or house? Was a particular person around when it occurred?

- Consider possible reasons why your Pomeranian may be misbehaving. Could your tone of voice be upsetting him? Was there a recent change in the household? Did someone go back to work? Is your Pom alone more frequently?

- Consult with your veterinarian for advice.

- Make a list of all of the possible solutions to the problem behavior.

- Go through your list of suggestions, and determine what will work best for you and your Pomeranian.

- Carry out the chosen solution. Be consistent and patient when doing so.

- Assess your results. If the problem is still occurring, you may need to contact a dog trainer or behavior expert.

Obedience training for your Pomeranian is a great way to prevent problems from occurring in the first place. Prevention is the key, especially since correcting bad behavior is much more challenging once the behavior is established. As the owner, it is your responsibility to ensure that you hold a leadership position, and obedience training can help establish you as the leader. If your position is not secure, you may find yourself being taken advantage of by your Pomeranian.

## Anxiety

Pomeranians can exhibit some poor behaviors as a result of various anxieties. This is why socialization is such an important thing to do with your Pomeranian. Failure to socialize can result in a Pomeranian with a crippling anxiety. Anxiety is often seen in puppy mill rescue Pomeranians—dogs who have had little or no human contact at all.

If your Pomeranian is already an anxious dog, you need to take steps right away to get him to overcome his fear. For example, if he is afraid of strangers, you can begin by bringing a "stranger" (one of your friends) over to your home. Don't let your friend approach the dog, let your Pom initiate the contact. Have your friend give the dog a treat. Be sure he has a safe hideaway he can retreat to if he feels overwhelmed. It is important to remember to start small and reward him for good behavior.

Through steady exposure, you should notice that he is relaxing more, as things become more familiar. If you

*The Expert Knows*

### When to Seek Professional Help

If you and your Pomeranian have attended obedience training classes and he still exhibits unwanted or problem behaviors, it is time to consult with your veterinarian and determine if he has a medical or a behavioral problem. Any problem that makes you feel uncomfortable should be addressed immediately—ignoring problems will not make them go away.

take him down a busy street, and he is scared, take him to a park to play, or a walk down a quiet street so that he does not fear the outings. While he may never learn to like being out in busy areas, he can learn to tolerate it.

## Noise Anxiety

Another anxiety which can lead to behavior problems is noise anxiety. Severe noise anxiety can be reduced by constant exposure. It's important to tackle the problem early on, so that you and your Pomeranian won't suffer every time there is a loud noise. The first step in dealing with this anxiety is to find out exactly what types of noises

*Exercise can help alleviate some problem behaviors.*

make him anxious. Many dogs are afraid of thunder, but other noises like the rumble of a train going by, a low airplane, loud bangs, or deep voices can also cause noise anxiety.

Try to remain calm during these situations. Sometimes owners unknowingly encourage their dog's fear reaction by getting upset and paying more attention to him, which makes him more fearful. Then ask your trainer or behaviorist to help you come up with a desensitization plan that's right for your Pomeranian. In extreme cases, there are medications that can help with thunderphobia (fear of thunder). You can discuss that option with your vet.

## Separation Anxiety

Pomeranians are meant to be companion animals and absolutely adore their owners. Sometimes this need for human contact can turn into separation anxiety—a disorder where a dog acts out with undesirable behavior when left alone. Signs include:

- Your dog gets overly excited when you leave or return home.
- Your dog doesn't eat while you are out of the house.
- Your dog follows you around constantly when you are home.
- Housesoiling and destructive behavior when you are gone.

Mild cases of separation anxiety can be helped by doing the following:

- Make your departure and arrival a routine. Encourage your Pomeranian to realize that your departures and arrivals are not out of the norm and, thus, are nothing to get excited over. Usually he feels the greatest amount of anxiety shortly after you leave, so practicing coming and going for a short period of time when he is a puppy will help him adjust to longer periods without you.

## Training the Older Pomeranian With Problem Behaviors

The first rule when training an older Pomeranian is to be patient. It is a good idea to consult with a veterinarian behaviorist as soon as possible so you can ensure you're on the right track from the start. Physical limitations should always be taken into account when training your older Pomeranian. A puppy has a much larger capacity for running, jumping, retrieval, and obstacle course maneuvers than a senior one.

Take training sessions in shorter time chunks, and expect them to be more repetitive. It is important to allow for longer recovery periods between sessions so he won't put too much strain on his body.

Refrain from over-treating your senior Pomeranian. He can gain weight more swiftly than his younger counterparts. It is important to offer rewards to him; just limit the number of times and quantity of each treat.

Keep in mind that if your older Pomeranian doesn't respond to you from a distance he may be suffering from hearing loss and not simply ignoring your calls.

- Give him lots of exercise. Exercise relieves stress. A long walk, run, or play session prior to leaving can really help to reduce the stress and anxiety your Pomeranian may experience.
- Give your Pomeranian something to do while you're gone, like leaving a toy stuffed with treats. If he has something entertaining to do while you are away, he will be less likely to become stressed and anxious.
- Confine him while you are gone. Some Pomeranians are more comfortable being confined to their own space. A crate can be an ideal space for your Pomeranian while you are away, or as an alternative confine him to one room.
- Set aside special time for your Pomeranian. Make time during your day to give him your undivided attention.
- Leave the radio or television on. This will allow him to hear voices and thus feel less lonely.

If your Pomeranian's anxiety seems severe, you will need to consult your veterinarian and/or a veterinary behaviorist.

## Barking (Excessive)

Owners of Pomeranians will tell you—their dogs have a resounding bark and do so quite often. This is a "barky" breed. Pomeranians bark during play, for attention, to communicate, and to alert you if a stranger is at the door or someone is passing your house on foot.

87

Barking is a natural behavior for dogs—they are trying to communicate with you! So to expect no barking at all, especially from a breed like a Pomeranian, is not practical. There are times, however, when it can turn into a problem. When is barking considered a problem? Problem barking is generally defined as barking constantly for a period of half an hour or more.

You need to determine the cause of his excessive barking before taking steps to reduce it. The two most common reasons Pomeranians bark for prolonged periods of time are boredom and loneliness. If your Pom is left alone for long periods and the neighbors have mentioned his excessive barking, make sure when you are home you play with him, take him for a long walks, and keep him near the family. He is most likely barking because he wants to be with you.

If your Pom is barking excessively when you aren't there, here are some tips to help you deal with it:

- Keep him in the crate while you are gone (not more than 4 hours at a time).

*Pomeranians were bred as companion dogs and need daily attention.*

- Leave the radio or television on—the sound of voices can help comfort him and make him feel less lonely.

- Give him something to occupy him while you are gone. Toys that hide treats inside can be very entertaining for him.

- You might want to sign him up for doggy daycare or have a dog sitter come by your house for a few hours while you are out.

If your dog is barking excessively while you are home, you'll want to start training him so he'll understand when enough barking is enough. It is important to teach him that it's okay to bark a few times when the doorbell rings or visitors stop by, but he needs to stop. You can do this by teaching him "Bark/No bark." Have some treats handy, and in a situation when he's naturally barking say "bark." When he stops on his own volition, say "No bark," give him a treat and praise. Any time he quiets down (e.g., after the doorbell has rung) say "Good, no bark" and give him a treat. He'll soon learn the rewards of being quiet.

## Chewing

All puppies need to chew—chewing eases teething discomfort, is a form of play, is a way to explore the environment, assuages hunger, establishes dominance, and relieves boredom. Many dogs carry this behavior over into adulthood—after all, it just plain feels good! But chewing can be a huge problem if your dog is chewing on inappropriate items. When my Pomeranian was a puppy he chewed through a lamp cord and got an electric shock. Fortunately, he was not seriously injured, but my family and I made sure to start hiding cords where he couldn't get to them, and sprayed bitter apple on the parts that showed. (Pierre is pretty smart though—after that harrowing experience he never chewed on anything other than a bone again!)

To help solve chewing problems, make sure your Pom has appropriate toys he can chew on. This can be a little challenging because of your Pomeranian's small mouth. Chewable bones and knotted ropes are available in small sizes; socks can be a great alternative if the smaller toys are difficult to locate (although if you do give him a sock, keep in mind he won't know the difference between his "toy" sock and your new ones).

### Finding a Behaviorist

There are times when you may need the help of a behaviorist. These are people who have studied and are knowledgeable about animal behavior. There are veterinarians with a special interest in behavior and veterinary behaviorists. To be considered by the American Veterinary Medical Society (AVMS) as a veterinarian behaviorist, you must have been inducted into the American College of Veterinary Behaviorists (ACVB) and successfully completed a residency program in veterinarian animal behavior and passed a certifying exam.

To find a behaviorist start with your veterinarian. He or she should be able to refer you to a behavior specialist. When you meet the behaviorist, be sure to ask questions—what are the training methods used? How long are the appointments? What will you/we be doing? How much will it cost? With the help of the specialist, you should be on your way to helping your Pom overcome any problem.

## FAMILY-FRIENDLY TIP
### Teaching Safety

You've taught your child to how to respectfully treat a dog. He or she knows how to pet gently, not yell and scream, and never hit the dog. Teaching your child how to treat a pet can avert many potential problems and misunderstandings. However, if your dog is showing any signs of a serious behavior problem, it is best to keep small children away from him while seeking professional help.

Make sure you play with your Pomeranian often so he will not be inclined to "play" with the furniture. If he is gnawing on the legs of your coffee table, there are bitter-tasting furniture sprays available, which can be very effective without being harmful to him.

Prevention is important to help stop chewing. Don't leave shoes, children's toys, or other items on the floor in easy reach of your puppy's eager mouth. Confine your Pomeranian to a crate when you cannot watch him, and make sure he has a toy in the crate that he is allowed to chew.

If you do find him chewing on something inappropriate, use discipline not punishment—say a stern "no" and remove the item from his mouth; then remove him to a neutral area and give him something he is allowed to chew on.

If your puppy is chewing on your hand, you'll also want to stop that behavior as soon as it starts. When he begins to chew, give him a sharp, "No," then turn your back on him. Soon, your Pom will learn that chewing on your hand means he doesn't get to play with you—one of his favorite things to do! Be persistent and consistent with your training. After all, if it was wrong yesterday, it's wrong today.

## Digging

Digging is a highly enjoyable and natural activity for dogs. If your Pomeranian loves digging, provide him with his own digging pit—just as parents would provide their child with a sandbox. Take some of his favorite dog toys and let him watch you bury them. Call him over and help him dig them up. Whenever he goes to his pit, treat and praise him.

Once he understands that digging in his pit is an acceptable and enjoyable activity, you can teach him that digging elsewhere is not. To do this, you'll have to keep an eye on him when he's outside. If he begins digging somewhere you don't want, say "No dig!" sharply, pick him up, and place him in his own digging pit. When he digs there, praise him.

## Housesoiling

Toy dogs are notoriously hard to housetrain, but with patience and consistency, it can be done. However, if your Pomeranian reaches four or five months of age and is still having regular accidents in the house, or if your adult Pom suddenly reverts in his housetraining, check with your veterinarian to make sure your dog does not have a bladder infection, intestinal parasites, or other medical reasons for housesoiling. Also, some spayed female Pomeranians will develop bladder incontinence as they age. This is not a housetraining problem and will normally be noticed as loss of urine where she is resting—she may not even be aware when it happens. This problem is easily controlled with inexpensive medication from your veterinarian.

If your vet gives your Pom a clean bill of health, you'll need to figure out why your dog may have begun eliminating inside. One reason may be that you are not recognizing your dog's signals to go out. Or, you may not be

*Give your dog lots of appropriate chew items.*

home when he does need to go (remember, Pom's have tiny bladders—even adults can't hold it as long as some bigger dogs). If you think this may be the case, you might want to paper train your Pomeranian to keep him from soiling in the house. The paper method works better with a puppy than with an adult Pomeranian, although it can be used on both. To begin, first you must choose a location where your Pom can eliminate, like a laundry room or small bathroom. Make sure the room is puppy-proofed and that eliminating on the floor in this area will not cause significant damage. Once you have chosen an area, cover the entire floor with newspaper.

When you notice signs that he needs to relieve himself, take him to the paper-covered room. When he has established his preferred spot, begin removing the paper from the rest of the room and only cover the area he has been using. Make sure you leave the papered area large enough so that he won't miss. When he uses that papered area, praise and/or reward him. The more your Pomeranian associates a reward with eliminating on the paper the quicker he will be trained to use it. Critics of paper training say that it only teaches your dog to continue eliminating inside the house. But by training him to only eliminate in one spot, many toy dog owners have used paper training successfully.

One other solution may be to have a dog sitter come by the house during the day, to give your Pom more opportunities to relieve himself outside.

## Finding a Lost Dog

No one wants to think about it, but it can happen—your Pom squeezes through a hole in the fence or dashes out the open front door and is gone! Hopefully this will never happen to you, but if it does, here's how to increase your chances of getting him back:

- Your best bet to get your dog back is to make sure he's easily identified with tags on his collar or a microchip. License numbers are on record in your local government office, and chips are registered with local or national databases.
- Place a lost dog ad in the daily newspapers.
- Let your veterinarian and his or her office staff know.
- Call animal shelters—not only in your immediate area, but in adjoining towns.
- Actually visit the public shelters every day or two—not all volunteers know what a Pomeranian looks like.
- Always keep an updated photo of your dog handy—make sure it's a good, clear shot.
- Make some posters with a color picture of your pet and post them around the neighborhood, in convenience stores, near schools.
- Knock on doors in your neighborhood and hand out flyers (keep your safety in mind, please!).

Jumping up is natural for the energetic Pom.

## Jumping Up

Jumping is normal dog behavior, especially for your Pomeranian. Because Pomeranians are such friendly dogs, they love to jump up on people's legs and jump onto someone's lap. He'll most likely engage in this behavior unless he is taught not to do so. While having a small dog like your Pom jumping up on someone may not seem like much of a threat, there are times when it's not appropriate (wearing that great new dress), and there are people who may be scared of your dogs (yes, even your adorable little Pomeranian).

The best way to train your Pomeranian not to jump up is to teach him a more acceptable alternative behavior, like the sit command. When your Pomeranian rushes to greet you when you return home, have a treat ready and say, "sit!" If he jumps up, turn your back and ignore him. When he sits, give him the treat and praise him.

# Chapter 8

# Stepping Out

There is more to life with your Pomeranian than grooming, taking him to the veterinarian, feeding, and training. Showing your Pomeranian, teaching him tricks, playing games, and traveling are all great ways to build your relationship while having fun together. Remember, your Pomeranian is a friendly, loving, enthusiastic, and energetic dog. Here are some great ways to encourage his playful and inquisitive nature.

## Agility

The fastest growing dog sport in the world is agility. Every breed can participate, including your Pomeranian. This fun, fast-paced sport is a timed race through an obstacle course that consists of tunnels, weave poles, jumps, seesaws, and more. The dog runs the course off lead, while the handler runs next to him and directs him with verbal and hand signals.

There are several different agility classes, and each offers increasing levels of difficulty in order to earn Novice, Open, and Excellent titles. The highest honor an agility dog can receive is to achieve a Master Agility Championship title (MACH).

Agility is lots of fun, but finding a place to train can be difficult, since the obstacles can take up a lot of room. Once nice thing about your pint-sized Pom, however, is that some of the training can actually take place in your house. I know one owner of a little dog who weighted the cardboard centers of paper towels, placed them down her hallway, and taught her little dog to weave through them!

## Canine Freestyle

Canine Freestyle is a choreographed performance with music that you and your Pomeranian can do together. In order to dance to music with your Pomeranian, there are some simple steps you need to follow. First select the music which you would like to dance to. Next, choreograph a routine to the music. The moves can be comprised of basic obedience steps, tricks, or any new step you create. It is important to plan the steps and movements within a defined area. You

*Examples of agility obstacles, including jumps and tunnels.*

may also want to select and coordinate clothing for you and your Pomeranian.

Once you have completed those basic steps, you now have a musical canine freestyle performance that you can perform for family and friends or take to a competition event. At a competition, there is a fourth step you must consider—meeting the rules/guidelines defined by the governing (musical) canine freestyle organization.

You can contact the World Canine Freestyle Organization or the Canine Freestyle Federation to find events, contacts, and classes in your area.

## Canine Good Citizen

The Canine Good Citizen (CGC) Program is designed to reward dogs who have good manners at home and in the community. It stresses responsible pet ownership for owners and basic good manners for dogs. The CGC test includes the following:

- Test 1: Accepting a friendly stranger
- Test 2: Sitting politely for petting
- Test 3: Appearance and grooming
- Test 4: Out for a walk (walking on a loose lead)
- Test 5: Walking through a crowd
- Test 6: Sit and down on command and Staying in place
- Test 7: Coming when called
- Test 8: Reaction to another dog
- Test 9: Reaction to distraction
- Test 10: Supervised separation

*The sport of obedience takes a lot of time and training.*

All dogs are eligible to participate. The CGC Program is often the first step to becoming a certified therapy dog.

## Obedience

Obedience is a sport which demonstrates your Pomeranian's ability to follow specified routines in the obedience ring. Depending on the level of difficulty of the trial, your dog will be asked to heel in a "pattern" as told to you by the judge. You will be asked to do right turns, left turns, about turns, slow, normal, and fast paces, and halts. These maneuvers are performed both on and off leash. There are also stay and recall exercises that challenge your Pom's ability to listen and perform commands.

Stepping Out

### Rally-O (Rally Obedience)

Rally obedience is a slightly looser, more fun version of traditional obedience. In rally, the dog and handler complete a course of designated stations that include instructions for performing a skill. A perfect heel is not required, and the handler is allowed to praise, talk, clap, and use any means of verbal communication to encourage his or her dog. Rally is a great way to develop teamwork with your dog and can promote fun and enjoyment for dogs at all levels of competition.

### Showing (Conformation)

Dog showing is a sport that has been around for over 100 years. The purpose behind dog shows is to judge the best examples of the breed for breeding stock. And how are these dogs judged? Each breed is compared to his breed standard—the written description of the breed that describes the ideal dog. The standard is written by the breed club and submitted to the national club for approval; only those breeds with approved standards can compete in events.

Pomeranians' intelligence and passion for attention make them great show dogs. Originally the breed had two size classes for showing: over 8 pounds (3.6 kg) and under 8 pounds. The smaller-sized Poms became so popular that the larger sizes stopped winning and then stopped being entered. Eventually that category was dropped altogether. Several years later the

## Sports and Safety

Always remember that your Pomeranian is small and rather fragile so chose sports and games that are size-appropriate and not too rough. If he jumps too far and/or hard, he can easily injure his legs or hips.

Pomeranian standard was revised to set the upper weight limit at 7 pounds (3.2 kg) where it remains to this day.

### How Dog Shows Work

What happens in the show ring? Sometimes you'll see all the same breed competing against each other. Other times you'll see different breeds in the same ring competing. Shows start out with "classes"—puppies and adult dogs of the same breed, males first, then females. The final class in a breed show determines the best of breed— the dog that most closely matches the breed standard.

Then that best in breed winner goes on to compete against others in his

Pomeranians

group. The national club divides dogs by groups, depending on their original function. For instance, the American Kennel Club has seven groups: Toy (that's where your Pom falls!), Terrier, Hound, Sporting, Working, Non-sporting, and Herding. The Kennel Club in England also has seven groups, but breaks them down differently: Hound, Working, Terrier, Gundog, Pastoral, Utility, and Toy.

Most of the most popular shows are aired on cable channels.

Once the Group winner has been chosen, the big finale comes—Best in Show! The judges are not comparing one dog to another (after all, how could anyone compare a Pomeranian to Great Dane?) but rather comparing each breed to the breed standard, and deciding which one comes the closest.

## Getting Started

If you are interested in showing your Pomeranian, you should attend several shows as a spectator. Study the judges and the way the handlers work with the dogs. You can request to read the judges score sheets and look at the comments made on each dog.

You should also talk to the Pomeranian owners involved in the shows, read dog magazines, and check out books on showing. Next, try to find a handling class. You can locate one by finding the kennel clubs in your area. By contacting the kennel clubs you can not only find handling classes, but find experienced show people who can help answer questions.

## Therapy

Therapy dogs are ones trained to provide affection and comfort to

*Show dogs must come as close as possible to the breed standard in order to win.*

BEST OF BREED

GILBERT PHOTO

**FAMILY-FRIENDLY TIP**

A great way to bring your child and your Pomeranian together is to get them involved in Junior Showmanship events. These events teach kids about dog shows, help them develop their dog handling skills, and learn about good sportsmanship.

The more kids know about dogs, the better their relationship with them. By putting time and effort into learning about their Pomeranian and how to present him at a show, juniors can be rewarded not only with ribbons, but also a lasting connection with the family dog.

people in hospitals, retirement homes, nursing homes, mental institutions, schools, and stressful situations such as disaster areas. Animals have been known to help people cope with traumatic events, lower blood pressure, improve general cardiovascular health, reduce stress, help curb loneliness, and lower the risk of allergies in children.

In order to qualify as a therapy dog, your Pomeranian must meet the following criteria:

- Be at least one year of age
- Have up-to-date vaccinations, be

well groomed, and parasite free

- Must be obedience trained and respond to basic commands
- Should be stable, have a tolerant temperament, and be free of any signs of aggression toward people or other dogs
- Must be able to handle new environments and a reasonable amount of stress (tolerant of loud noises, sudden movements, etc.)
- Must be registered with a recognized dog therapy organization

There are a number of organizations involved in the preparation and registration of therapy dogs. Therapy Dogs International, Therapy Dogs Inc., and the Delta Society are examples of such groups. Upon registering with one of these organizations, your Pomeranian will be put through the tests associated with the Canine Good Citizen certificate mentioned earlier in this chapter. Once he has passed and received his certificate, you and your Pomeranian will be trained to participate in programs at hospitals, nursing homes, rehabilitation centers, and schools. Participation as a therapy dog and volunteer can be quite rewarding to both you and your Pomeranian. Since Poms are social dogs, they will enjoy the interaction and companionship, and those visited will revel in his adorable looks and pleasant nature.

*The Pomeranian's size and happy nature make him a great therapy dog.*

Tracking requires very little equipment. You just need a harness, a 20-to-40 foot (6 to 12 m) lead, a few flags to mark your track, and an open grassy area free of obstacles such as roads, ditches, or woods.

At a tracking event, your dog will be asked to track an article (like a leather glove) that has been dragged along the ground. You then follow the dog on the long lead.

A dog can earn three AKC Tracking titles; each has an increased degree of difficulty: TD (Tracking Dog); TDX (Tracking Dog Excellent); or VST (Variable Surface Tracker) title. A Champion Tracker (CT) is awarded only to those dogs that have earned all three tracking titles.

## Tracking

Tracking is a canine sport that demonstrates a dog's natural ability to recognize and follow a scent; it is the foundation of canine search and rescue work. Tracking is open to all breeds; however, some have more of a natural aptitude and enjoyment of this sport than others. If your little dog's idea of a good time is lounging on your lap inside on a cold day, tracking may not be for him. But some Pomeranians are hearty little dogs who love the outdoor nature of this sport.

## Traveling

When traveling, you have several options: taking your Pomeranian with you, boarding him, or having someone care for him in your home. Let's discuss boarding first.

## Boarding Kennels

Boarding kennels can be divided into two categories: those that provide basic care and those that offer more upscale amenities. Visit the kennel first before sending your Pomeranian there. Ask questions, talk to the kennel staff, and make sure the kennel:

- Has indoor-outdoor runs or indoor runs and an exercise plan.
- Hoses the runs every day (dogs are outside when inside runs are cleaned, and inside when outside runs are cleaned).
- Cleans with disinfectant.
- Provides good ventilation.
- Makes provisions for a variety of diets.
- Feeds your dog on his own schedule with his own diet.
- Provides some sort of bedding to keep the dog off the concrete floor.
- Keeps bedding clean.
- Gives any necessary medications.
- Contacts your dog's veterinarian if necessary and gives a bit of extra attention to old dogs.
- Checks the dogs several times daily to make sure they are well.
- Requires that pets are current on all vaccinations, including Bordatella vaccination

Most Pomeranians do well in a kennel with indoor-outdoor runs, feedings twice a day, and a caring staff that pays close attention to them. To prepare your Pomeranian for his stay at a

kennel, make sure his health check, vaccinations, and heartworm medication are up-to-date. Also make sure he is flea-free. If your Pomeranian is on a special diet, make sure you bring it with you.

## Pet Sitters

Pet sitters can be a great alternative to a boarding kennel when you travel or leave your Pomeranian at home alone while you work. Some advantages to having a pet sitter come to you home are:

- Your Pomeranian will be happier and experience less stress if he stays in his own home.
- His diet and exercise routines will be uninterrupted.
- Travel trauma for both you and your Pomeranian is eliminated.
- Your Pomeranian's exposure to

*Make sure the boarding kennel is clean and well-kept.*

other dogs' illnesses is minimized.

- There is no need to call untrained or unwilling friends/family/neighbors to look after him.

However, finding a good, trustworthy pet sitter can be as much as a challenge as finding a dependable babysitter. When choosing a pet sitter make sure they provide you with insurance and personal references. You should receive and sign a written service contract. Make sure the pet sitter responds to your questions, concerns, and complaints properly and that a plan is in place for emergencies or bad weather. You should meet with the prospective pet sitter and your Pomeranian together and watch how they interact. If your Pomeranian responds well, and the pet sitter asks you important questions and has adequate training, he or she may be the right match for you.

## Taking Your Pomeranian With You

One great advantage to having such a small dog is that he's perfectly portable! Before you start on any trip with your dog, be sure to check pet policies when making reservations at motels, hotels, inns, lodges, or campgrounds.

Traveling with your Pomeranian requires forethought and planning. The best thing you can do prior to traveling with him is to see your veterinarian. He

## SENIOR DOG TIP

### Traveling With an Older Pomeranians

Older dogs can be great travel companions. Just avoid putting an older dog in the cargo section of an airplane. If for some reason your senior Pom can't fly in the cabin with you, you're better off leaving him at home. Check out the options for boarding and pet sitting earlier in this chapter—they might be the right thing to do for your senior dog.

or she can determine if your Pomeranian will be able to withstand the strain of a trip and what kinds of precautions you will need to take.

### By Car

Whether you are heading out to do errands or going on a long trip, there are a number of ways your Pomeranian can join in the car that are both safe and comfortable. A dog riding unrestrained in a car or truck is dangerous—a loose dog is a distraction, and he will have no protection in case of an accident. Your dog should not be allowed to ride with his head outside car windows. Particles of dirt can enter his eyes and nose,

## What to Pack

Your travel kit should include:
- crate
- first-aid kit
- familiar toys
- supply of his regular food and treats
- at least two six-foot leashes and a retractable leash if desired
- a spare collar
- food and water bowls
- water bottle
- proof of license and vaccination
- brush or comb
- recent photograph for identification in case he gets lost
- identification tag attached firmly to his collar

causing injury or infection.

The best way to ensure his safety is to confine him. There are seat belts available for dogs. They come in different sizes and work with a harness piece that goes over the chest and attaches to the car's seat belt. Smaller dogs can also fit into car seats made specifically for dogs. They not only provide safety but can be raised or lowered to allow your Pom to see out the window.

Another option for restraining your Pomeranian inside a car is a crate. Portable crates are comfortable for your Pomeranian, and if he's already crate trained it probably won't be hard to get him used to traveling in one. Start by taking him on short trips in the beginning. Small carriers can usually be secured to the seat using the car's seat belt.

On rare occasions, your Pomeranian may become car sick. You'll need to try to acclimate him slowly to riding in the car. Put him in the car for a few minutes each day without going anywhere. Then when he's calm, drive around the block, and once he's used to that, make the trips longer. You should build up the distance and time in the car gradually.

There are some over-the-counter medications you can try to help with carsickness. Ask your veterinarian about what might work and the correct dosage for your Pomeranian.

While on the road, use the air-conditioning to keep the car cool, and be sure to stop at rest areas every three to four hours so he can stretch his legs and relieve himself. Remember not to leave your Pomeranian in the car—even with the windows cracked. As Veterinarian Gail Golab notes, "Heat prostration is a common cause of summer illness that can, and does, kill many beloved pets each year." Your car

Inside a crate is a safe way for your Pom to travel.

heats up much quicker than you might realize, and leaving your Pom inside could be deadly.

## By Air

If you're planning to fly, federal guidelines require that your Pomeranian be at least eight weeks old. Your Pomeranian's vaccines should be up-to-date as well; a record of such should be available to show the airline.

Because your Pomeranian is so small, he should be allowed to travel as a carry-on in the cabin with you, which is much safer than checking him as baggage. Always check with the airline beforehand, as different carriers have different policies. Your dog must be restrained in a carrier, and the carrier must be small enough to fit under your seat. Be mindful of other passengers—if

you have a Pomeranian who enjoys barking (and most do), extra training to keep him from making too much noise should be in order.

One last tip to remember when traveling with your Pomeranian—he should wear identification of some sort at all times. The most common but least reliable is the license tag hanging from a hook on the collar, or you can invest in the more reliable microchip.

Here are some tips from the AKC when traveling with your Pomeranian:

- Make sure your Pomeranian has a reliable leash and collar which has identification tags, a license, proof of rabies vaccinations, and your telephone number.

- You may want to consider a microchip or tattoo that can increase the likelihood of finding your lost Pomeranian.

- Always carry recent pictures of your Pomeranian with you. If accidentally separated, they will help local authorities identify and locate him more swiftly.

- Remember to take your veterinarian's telephone number and any special medication he needs with you.

- It's not a good idea to change his diet while on a trip, so make sure to pack your Pomeranian's regular food and bowls (as well as plenty of water).

- Keep on hand current vaccination records.

105

Stepping Out

# Resources

## Associations and Organizations

### Breed Clubs

**American Kennel Club (AKC)**
5580 Centerview Drive
Raleigh, NC 27606
Telephone: (919) 233-9767
Fax: (919) 233-3627
E-mail: info@akc.org
www.akc.org

**Canadian Kennel Club (CKC)**
89 Skyway Avenue, Suite 100
Etobicoke, Ontario M9W 6R4
Telephone: (416) 675-5511
Fax: (416) 675-6506
E-mail: information@ckc.ca
www.ckc.ca

**Federation Cynologique
Internationale (FCI)**
Secretariat General de la FCI
Place Albert 1er, 13
B – 6530 Thuin
Belqique
www.fci.be

**The Kennel Club**
1 Clarges Street
London
W1J 8AB
Telephone: 0870 606 6750
Fax: 0207 518 1058
www.the-kennel-club.org.uk

**United Kennel Club (UKC)**
100 E. Kilgore Road
Kalamazoo, MI 49002-5584
Telephone: (269) 343-9020
Fax: (269) 343-7037
E-mail: pbickell@ukcdogs.com
www.ukcdogs.com

### Pet Sitters

**National Association of Professional
Pet Sitters**
15000 Commerce Parkway, Suite C
Mt. Laurel, New Jersey 08054
Telephone: (856) 439-0324
Fax: (856) 439-0525
E-mail: napps@ahint.com
www.petsitters.org

**Pet Sitters International**
201 East King Street
King, NC 27021-9161
Telephone: (336) 983-9222
Fax: (336) 983-5266
E-mail: info@petsit.com
www.petsit.com

### Rescue Organizations and Animal Welfare Groups

**American Humane Association (AHA)**
63 Inverness Drive East
Englewood, CO 80112
Telephone: (303) 792-9900
Fax: 792-5333
www.americanhumane.org

**American Society for the Prevention of Cruelty to Animals (ASPCA)**
424 E. 92nd Street
New York, NY 10128-6804
Telephone: (212) 876-7700
www.aspca.org

**Royal Society for the Prevention of Cruelty to Animals (RSPCA)**
Telephone: 0870 3335 999
Fax: 0870 7530 284
www.rspca.org.uk

**The Humane Society of the United States (HSUS)**
2100 L Street, NW
Washington DC 20037
Telephone: (202) 452-1100
www.hsus.org

## Sports

**Canine Freestyle Federation, Inc.**
Secretary: Brandy Clymire
E-Mail: secretary@canine-freestyle.org
www.canine-freestyle.org

**International Agility Link (IAL)**
Global Administrator: Steve Drinkwater
E-mail: yunde@powerup.au
www.agilityclick.com/~ial

**North American Dog Agility Council**
11522 South Hwy 3
Cataldo, ID 83810
www.nadac.com

**United States Dog Agility Association**
P.O. Box 850955
Richardson, TX 75085-0955
Telephone: (972) 487-2200
www.usdaa.com

**World Canine Freestyle Organization**
P.O. Box 350122
Brooklyn, NY 11235-2525
Telephone: (718) 332-8336
www.worldcaninefreestyle.org

## Therapy

**Delta Society**
875 124th Ave NE, Suite 101
Bellevue, WA 98005
Telephone: (425) 226-7357
Fax: (425) 235-1076
E-mail: info@deltasociety.org
www.deltasociety.org

**Therapy Dogs Incorporated**
P.O. Box 5868
Cheyenne, WY 82003
Telephone: (877) 843-7364
E-mail: therdog@sisna.com
www.therapydogs.com

**Therapy Dogs International (TDI)**
88 Bartley Road
Flanders, NJ 07836
Telephone: (973) 252-9800
Fax: (973) 252-7171
E-mail: tdi@gti.net
www.tdi-dog.org

## Training

**Association of Pet Dog Trainers (APDT)**
150 Executive Center Drive Box 35
Greenville, SC 29615
Telephone: (800) PET-DOGS
Fax: (864) 331-0767
E-mail: information@apdt.com
www.apdt.com

## Vetrinary and Health Resources

**American Animal Hospital Association (AAHA)**
P.O. Box 150899
Denver, CO 80215-0899
Telephone: (303) 986-2800
Fax: (303) 986-1700
E-mail: info@aahanet.org
www.aahanet.org/index.cfm

**American Holistic Veterinary Medical Association (AHVMA)**
2218 Old Emmorton Road
Bel Air, MD 21015
Telephone: (410) 569-0795
Fax: (410) 569-2346
E-mail: office@ahvma.org
www.ahvma.org

**American Veterinary Medical Association (AVMA)**
1931 North Meacham Road – Suite 100
Schaumburg, IL 60173
Telephone: (847) 925-8070
Fax: (847) 925-1329
E-mail: avmainfo@avma.org
www.avma.org

**ASPCA Animal Poison Control Center**
1717 South Philo Road, Suite 36
Urbana, IL 61802
Telephone: (888) 426-4435
www.aspca.org

**British Veterinary Association (BVA)**
7 Mansfield Street
London
W1G 9NQ
Telephone: 020 7636 6541
Fax: 020 7436 2970
E-mail: bvahq@bva.co.uk
www.bva.co.uk

**Canine Eye Registration Foundation (CERF)**
VMDB/CERF
1248 Lynn Hall
625 Harrison St.
Purdue University
West Lafayette, IN 47907-2026
Telephone: (765) 494-8179
E-mail: CERF@vmbd.org
www.vmdb.org

**Orthopedic Foundation for Animals (OFA)**
2300 NE Nifong Blvd
Columbus, Missouri 65201-3856
Telephone: (573) 442-0418
Fax: (573) 875-5073
Email: ofa@offa.org
www.offa.org

# Index

Pomeranians

**111**

## Dedication

This book is dedicated to Abigail, whose love of animals—especially Pierre—serves as a reminder of how precious even our smallest family members are.

## Acknowledgements

I would like to thank my husband, Mark, for his input on, experiences with, and love for his Pomeranian.

I would like to thank the AKC and their hard workers for guiding me in all the right directions, the staff at the *Pom Reader* for sharing their stories, experiences, and resources, and Heather Russell-Revesz of TFH Publications for her fantastic editing skills.

I would also like to thank Pierre for the love, memories and smiles he has brought our family over the years.

## About the Author

Marguerite Stocker is a published poet and a manager of the Brookdale Community College Bookstore in Monmouth County, New Jersey. A graduate from Boston University's School of Communication, she is currently in the process of finishing her master's degree in Business from Thomas Edison State College. She lives in Red Bank, New Jersey with her husband, daughter, Pomeranian, and two cats.

## PHOTO CREDITS

Larry Allen: 93
Christine Bork (Shutterstock): 70
Paulette Braun: 12
Linda Bucklin (Shutterstock): 50, 58
Elaine Davis (Shutterstock): 72
Theresa Martinez (Shutterstock): 96
Patricia Marroquin (Shutterstock): 10
Tammy McAllister (Shutterstock): 18
N. Silcock (Shutterstock): 17 (bottom)

Christina Reid (Shutterstock): 36
revelationmedia (Shutterstock): 84
Lauren Rinder (Shutterstock): 74
Chin Kit Sen (Shutterstock): 49
April Turner (Shutterstock): 15
WizData, Inc. (Shutterstock): 4
All other photos courtesy of Isabelle Francais
Cover photo: Candace Schwadron (Shutterstock)